Gen Z

Gen Z is a vital, thought-provoking portrait of an astonishing generation. Drawing on first-hand interviews and empirical evidence, it offers insight into the boom in political activism amongst those born post-2000, exploring its roots and wide implications for the future of our society.

As environmental disaster threatens the fundamental existence and livelihoods of Generation Z, this book considers how the fact that they have taken up the fight is likely to be one of the best things that could have happened to them. Focusing on the school climate change strikes and Greta Thunberg as initiator and icon of the Fridays for Future movement, it reveals the evolving world of Gen Z at school, at work, at home and online. It documents the development of their politicisation, the challenges they and their activism face in light of the global pandemic and considers how the experience of those on the margins can differ from their peers.

Gen Z is a compelling study of how fighting the climate crisis is only the beginning for these young people. It offers insight for all those interested in the study of adolescence and emerging adulthood, as well as teachers, youth workers, civil society activists, policymakers, politicians and parents who want to understand young people's aspirations for the future.

Klaus Hurrelmann is Senior Professor of Social Sciences at the Hertie School of Governance in Berlin, Germany.

Erik Albrecht is a freelance radio journalist and international media development expert based in Berlin, Germany.

Gen Z

Between Climate Crisis and
Coronavirus Pandemic

Klaus Hurrelmann
and Erik Albrecht

Translated by
Angelika Behlen,
Dayna Sadow and
Julia Sittmann

Routledge
Taylor & Francis Group

LONDON AND NEW YORK

First published 2021
by Routledge
2 Park Square, Milton Park, Abingdon, Oxon OX14 4RN

and by Routledge
605 Third Avenue, New York, NY 10158

Routledge is an imprint of the Taylor & Francis Group, an informa business

© 2021 Klaus Hurrelmann and Erik Albrecht

British Library Cataloguing-in-Publication Data
A catalogue record for this book is available from the British Library

Library of Congress Cataloging-in-Publication Data
A catalog record has been requested for this book

ISBN: 978-0-367-65279-1 (hbk)
ISBN: 978-0-367-65280-7 (pbk)
ISBN: 978-1-003-12870-0 (ebk)

Typeset in Bembo
by Taylor & Francis Books

Contents

Introduction

"We are young, we are here, we want a future without fear!"[1] – a slogan that brought hundreds of thousands of mostly young people onto the streets in Germany and elsewhere for much of 2019. By that summer, the Fridays for Future movement had already succeeded in putting the climate crisis on the agenda of governments across the world. Only the coronavirus pandemic could bring the wave of public protests to an abrupt halt in March 2020. Nonetheless, the issue – and their protest – remains: The environmental movement Fridays for Future has managed to unite tens of thousands of young people worldwide in the fight against the climate crisis.

Anyone who takes the time to talk to young people today about what is important to them will hear a similar refrain: "I'm afraid of what the earth will look like in 100 years," says 12-year-old Friedrich at a Berlin middle school. "I think it's important that we, as the young generation, stand up and say: 'No, stop, you can't go on like this! We want a planet, too,'" adds Markus only a few months before graduating from high school in Frankfurt an der Oder, a medium-sized town nestled in the Polish-German border region.

While Generation X, (here defined as those born between 1970 and 1985), and Generation Y, the oft-maligned "millennials" born after 1985, were very much "me" generations, interested more in their own well-being and securing a professional existence than in considering the collective needs of their society, the post-millennials, usually referred to as Generation Z, are different. Currently coming of age, Generation Z – born after the turn of the millennium – is considerably more interested and active in politics than many of the cohorts that preceded it. An unusually large number of them are actively engaged in political life, social change and community activism. The coronavirus pandemic has done little to dampen their motivation and enthusiasm.

In contrast to their elders, Gen Z is also considerably less happy with the state of our societies. Their main concern, according to youth studies: Almost no government in the world has met its obligations under the Paris climate agreement to reduce overall global warming by 1.5 degrees. In this regard, Germany is a striking example: In 2005, Chancellor Angela Merkel began her first of four terms in office as the "climate chancellor" with the ultimate goal of reducing the country's climate carbon emissions to a sustainable level. 15 years later, she has achieved hardly any of her self-imposed climate objectives.

As a result, young people are losing confidence in both politicians and party politics. The more dedicated among this generation now feel that they must take matters into their own hands, firmly convinced that current politicians are in no position to be setting the course for *their* futures. From their perspective, politics has become lost in the trivialities of daily governance, moving too slowly, too cautiously, and invariably in the interests of large corporations and lobby groups. And now, as the coronavirus pandemic rages, all decisions about the future are treated as secondary to managing the impact of this global health crisis anyway.

The younger generation is no longer willing to tolerate this procrastination. "When you think about 'the future' today, you don't think beyond the year 2050," according to Greta Thunberg, the Swedish schoolgirl born on 3 January 2003 who initiated the global climate movement Fridays for Future (FFF). "By then, I will, in the best case, not even have lived half of my life."[2]

It is this difference in perspective that has always made young people a seismograph for future developments. But never before have so many young people in so many countries taken to the streets at the same time to express their concerns on such a massive scale. Never have so many young people had the feeling that there is no time to waste. Many of them are scared and anxious about the future.

While the traditional political parties and their generally older voters seem to be caught up in the rigid procedures of political life, the younger generation has recognised the sign of the times. In this book, we want to analyse this change in political consciousness from one generation to the next. Why it is that two politically very reluctant generations, X and Y, whose members are now between the ages of 35 and 50 and 20 and 35 respectively, have been succeeded by a younger generation so much better able to speak their minds in a loud and critical fashion? We will show that it was and still is the young Swede, Greta Thunberg, who has influenced this generation with her climate protests, not only in her home country of Sweden, not only in Germany, where she has received a great deal of attention, but also in dozens of other countries around the world.

Only two years in, the restrictions on public life caused by the coronavirus pandemic have deprived the movement of the opportunity to take their struggle to the streets. During the initial lockdown phase beginning in March 2020, demonstrations were severely curtailed and schools shut down for months or allowed to function only under strict restrictions. Politically active adolescents and young adults, however, have not been silenced. They have made sure their voices are still heard across digital platforms, and, step by step, they are gathering again on Fridays to protest. While the coronavirus pandemic will likely recede eventually, the climate crisis is here to stay.

That being said, Generation Z is also a deeply polarised generation. The Fridays for Future movement only represents one part of Generation Z. In Germany, 40 percent of the young people involved in environmental activism come from affluent homes and are in the process of completing a solid education. At the other end of the social spectrum, almost a third of young women and – in particular – young men remain economically and educationally disadvantaged and feel discriminated against, unable to think about the future of the planet while their own future as working citizens is under threat by various forces.

One could say that Generation Z is mostly composed of members of a "Generation Greta," but this majority is under pressure due to the serious economic consequences of the coronavirus pandemic. If youth unemployment escalates, the current minority of disadvantaged and discriminated young people could rapidly increase, establishing a downtrodden "Generation Covid."

A meaningful consideration of the voices of the younger generation is vital for any functioning society – not only in Germany, the country selected as a case study for this book. A careful analysis of the attitudes and opinions of this generation is thus critically important: youth research is invariably a study of the future. Coming social and intellectual developments can be identified in youth studies long before they affect society at large. Young people, who still have so much of their lives ahead of them, are considerably more sensitive to future developments than older people in the middle or later stages of their lives. In addition, young people – most of whom have not (yet) accumulated much in the way of property or privilege to defend – have greater freedom to find creative solutions to longstanding problems. Those who see no chance for themselves will grasp at any straw.

With this book, we want to give a voice to the young generation, based on empirically sound studies and representative interviews. We use research-based youth studies, which use representative samples to trace the values, attitudes, characteristics and behavioural patterns of this generation. We complement these studies with personal interviews and participatory observation of young people that capture their authentic expressions and lived experiences. This allows us to illustrate how Generation Z lives and is influenced by the interplay between the climate crisis and the coronavirus pandemic, two ongoing issues which will likely deeply affect the rest of their still-young lives.

We would like to thank our research collaborators from the various studies on which this analysis is based as well as the teachers who generously shared their time and their expertise. Above all, we would like to pay tribute to the young people we interviewed, whose words give this book the authentic voice of their generation.

Klaus Hurrelmann
Erik Albrecht

Notes

1 Rough translation from the original German slogan: "*Wir sind hier, wir sind laut, weil ihr uns die Zukunft klaut!*"
2 Thunberg 2019, p. 25.

Chapter 1

The climate crisis is just the beginning
Who are the young protesters and what do they want?

Fridays for Future

"No life on Saturn," reads the poster Camilla holds up in dreary downtown Dortmund. Underneath: "Save the Earth now." The 20-something activist stands in front of a franchise of the popular electronics store bearing the same name on the city's main drag. About two dozen climate activists have donned makeshift costumes for the demonstration: A little glitter on their faces and gold foil from a cut-up thermal blanket on their heads has to suffice to identify them as aliens from another planet. While Dortmund grew rich on coal mining and the steel industry, the deindustrialisation of the second half of the last century has been deeply painful for many here.

While Camilla keeps vigil in front of the Saturn store, the rest of the group goes shopping. The store's one-man security team can do little to stop the rush of young people coming through the doors. With languid, space-like movements they slowly glide up the escalator to the upper floors and are soon dancing through the narrow aisles between coffee machines and hi-fi systems, calling on buyers and employees alike to go on climate strike. In the end, their call to action is displayed on computer screens throughout the store. In the drugstore next door, Camilla's fellow activists are ordered from the premises.

Since the summer of 2018, students across the world have demonstrated on nearly every Friday for the climate during the school year. In Germany, the first group met in Bad Segeberg, a small town in northern Germany, to engage in "political truancy": Instead of going to school, they went to the town hall to demonstrate with handmade posters and banners. A week later, about 300 students gathered in front of the Bundestag (the parliament building) in Germany's capital Berlin. "They all came without knowing what it would lead to," recalls Luisa Neubauer, one of the initiators, who was to become one of the most prominent faces of the protest in the following months. "Either success or just a wasted hour and trouble from parents and teachers."[1]

By 2019, the movement was spreading nationwide. Local groups quickly formed, often organised from within existing student councils at secondary schools. At the end of January 2019, 5,000 students gathered in Berlin for the Friday demonstrations and formed the movement Fridays for Future Germany (FFFD). On 1 March 2019, Greta Thunberg took part in a German demonstration for the first time – in Hamburg.

Today, FFFD is one of Germany's largest social movements, with about 600 local groups. Fridays for Future (FFF) has gained a foothold in almost every European country and has spread to other continents. By spring 2019, the movement had brought more than 1.6 million people onto the streets worldwide, and by autumn of that year, the number had almost doubled. Greta Thunberg, the icon of the movement, spoke in front of the EU Parliament, the World Economic Forum and the United Nations. No youth movement has ever received so much global attention.[2]

At the climate conference in Madrid in December 2019, FFF was present at every meeting venue. Young people arrived from every continent and loudly demonstrated – "What do we want? Climate justice!" – for speedy international agreements to stem the tide of this crisis. Once again, Greta Thunberg by her presence alone made it impossible for the delegates representing the 197 treaty countries to ignore the movement and its arguments.

In Germany, initial amazement about the new youth movement was quickly followed by a public debate on the question of "Don't they have to be at school?" The students, however, deliberately chose their form of protest; they are convinced that the government needed a wake-up call to finally take action on climate issues. It is, after all, their entire future that is at stake.

The use of school strikes as a targeted act of civil disobedience garnered overwhelming and unparalleled public attention for the demonstrations. Students copied Greta Thunberg's idea after she began picketing in front of the Swedish parliament in Stockholm every Friday instead of going to school.

In Germany, school attendance is compulsory until the age of 16, and home-schooling is illegal except in extraordinary circumstances (as the coronavirus pandemic illustrated a year later). When young people fail to attend class, the school administration formally records the absence. This absence does not appear on their report card as long as they submit a written statement from their legal guardians, usually their parents. If there are repeated absences, however, and a student does not provide a note from their parents, the police are usually called in. Parents can receive a warning or a fine for their children's unexcused absences.

In such a strictly regulated school system, school strikes involved numerous levels of authority: First, the parents, who had to write absence notes for their children, then the teachers, the school administration and the educational authorities. It also attracted the attention of the media, which granted extensive coverage to the strikes. "Skipping school" became a provocative means to an end and, soon enough, allowed the young activists to place their message at the centre of public debate, putting pressure on the government's climate policy.

Germany's energy policy has been up for vociferous debate since the West German anti-nuclear power movement entered the public consciousness in the 1970s. After the subsequent phase-out of nuclear energy, hopes were high that the country would use that momentum to become a global pioneer in the use of renewable energy sources – but these hopes were subsequently dashed.

In early 2019, FFF stepped into the gap between expectations and reality by loudly drawing attention to the government's failures. In its struggle to stop climate change, FFF has joined forces with many other – often more radical – environmental movements to fight against specific issues like the continued mining of lignite coal in the Lausitz region or the construction of new motorways in Hesse. While the Green Party's success in the 2019 European elections showed that it was possible to win elections based on climate and environmental policy, it was Fridays for Future that managed to place the climate crisis at the top of the political agenda. Suddenly, it became all too clear just how hollow, bland and insincere the policies of the two traditional mainstream parties – the reform-oriented Social Democratic Party (SPD) and the pair of conservative sister parties, Christian Democratic Union (CDU) and Christian Social Union (CSU) – were on the subject of the climate crisis.

Public attention was thus primed when, on 20 September 2019, FFF's climate activists called for a worldwide day of action. In cities across Germany – and across the world – smaller and larger groups came together to protest against government inaction on climate change. In Berlin alone, over 100,000 people of all ages and walks of life marched from the Brandenburg Gate to Alexanderplatz, a huge public square about three kilometres away. FFF estimated that 1.4 million demonstrators participated nationwide.

As people gathered in front of the Brandenburg Gate for the largest climate demonstration Berlin had ever seen, the German government's 'climate cabinet' was heading home for a change of clothes and a snack. Throughout the night, for almost 19 hours straight, they had struggled to negotiate a government package with measures to combat the climate crisis. In the end, the results were anything but the "great leap" that SPD Finance Minister Olaf Scholz had promised. Even business associations − alongside scientists, environmental associations and members of the opposition − criticised the measures as too feeble. Very few, even among the Fridays for Future activists, had expected the government to meet all of their demands, but the fact that the "climate package" would turn out to be such a small parcel was nonetheless a bitter pill for many.

Since then, it has seemed certain that Germany will not meet the climate targets set by the government for 2030. Nevertheless, since 20 September 2019, there is no longer a viable political path around the issue − which is considerably more than many previous movements have ever achieved. Indeed, a year later, in their attempt to forestall the impending collapse of the economy due to the coronavirus pandemic, the government adopted an economic stimulus package worth a staggering 130 billion euros that did not give in to efforts by lobbyists from the traditional industrial powerhouses to ignore environmental considerations in the face of economic necessity. On the contrary, in addition to a temporary reduction in the value added tax and a one-time bonus payment to parents of minors, programmes were introduced to encourage the improvement of public transport networks, the purchase of electric cars and the expansion of both the hydrogen economy and quantum technologies. The plan is for Germany to exit this crisis greener than it had entered it. Beyond that, another thing stands out: The young FFF activists have always called for quick, decisive action supported by scientific expertise, in contrast to politicians, who often argue that such action is simply too disruptive. In the wake of the pandemic, the government proved its own politicians wrong.

That being said, the shockwave of infections shifted public attention from the climate crisis to health issues overnight, creating a very real danger that the pandemic would blow away the young environmental movement. Large street demonstrations, FFF's most important trademark and organising strategy, were difficult or impossible to continue due to the lockdown and subsequent restrictions on the right of assembly. In addition, the provocative "school strike" completely lost its effect during the school closures, which lasted for weeks. Nevertheless, it has become clear that a politically active young generation has made an indelible mark on society, and many leading figures have pointed to the close connection between the climate crisis and the pandemic. The movement's most prominent speaker in Germany, Luisa Neubauer, argued in an interview with National Public Radio in June 2020:

The nature of the coronavirus crisis is completely different from the climate crisis. The climate crisis comes at you with less heft, but it requires more incisive action. [...] We can still learn a lot from the coronavirus crisis: We can take crises seriously. We can listen to science. We can come together internationally...we can make politics intergenerational.[3]

Throughout the pandemic, the movement has continued to emphasise the absolute priority of combating the climate crisis. In the meantime, it has been forced to get creative, by inventing new digital forms of protest and resuming small-scale rallies on Fridays in strict compliance with all social-distancing rules and hygiene regulations – and by expanding its field of action: It now openly supports other movements with different priorities. Following the murder of George Floyd by the police in Minneapolis (USA) at the end of May 2020, numerous FFF activists participated in the organisation of Black Lives Matter demonstrations. Their fight against climate change has transformed many in this generation into seasoned political actors – with the energy and stamina to stay the course.

Suddenly political?

When the bell rings in the late-nineteenth-century hallways of Sophie Scholl Secondary School in Berlin-Schöneberg, the doors to the classrooms fly open. The voices of more than a thousand students, from seventh to thirteenth grade, reverberate from the corridors' vaulted ceilings, as the building's staircases channel the masses to their next lesson. Everyday school life – on Fridays no less than on any other weekday.

Secondary schools such as Sophie School offer all three school leaving certifications – the basic qualification after nine, the intermediate qualification after ten, and the most advanced pre-university qualification (Abitur) after 12 or 13 years. Only some of the students attend the Fridays for Future protests in Berlin's Invalidenpark on a regular basis. "I'd like to go more often," says Adrian, an eight-grader. "But sometimes it doesn't work out. Last time, we had a test in class."

And yet environmentalism and climate change are ubiquitous in the hallways of the school. While the thick walls of the old building keep out the heat of a Central European summer with record temperatures, the Amazon is burning. Samira, a classmate of Adrian's, is horrified by Brazilian President Jair Bolsonaro's attitude on the issue. "He just can't understand what's going on," Adrian adds. "What is stupid is that he even refused to allow others to come in and help fight it."

Since Fridays for Future took off, Adrian's mother does not buy food in plastic packaging anymore; Adrian insists on it. But he also knows it is not enough. "That's pretty much it," he admits. "There's not much you can do as an individual," explains Adrian. "Politics has to change." In so doing, he is echoing one of the basic demands made by those young people taking to the streets. They know that individual sacrifices will not save the planet, which is why they want to see more regulation of polluting industries from politicians and the state. Whether industry and transportation, consumption and agriculture, building refurbishment or air travel – the message is that climate policy must affect all areas of our lives if we want to stop the climate crisis or at a minimum mitigate its consequences.

Young people are becoming more political again. And while this is true for virtually all highly developed countries, the shift is particularly noticeable in Germany. Whereas at the turn of the millennium, only one in three young people stated that they were interested in politics, today that figure has increased to just under one in two. It is also striking that the percentage of those who are "very" interested is particularly high. The last time young people were more interested in politics than now was in 1991 – the era of German reunification, during which 57 percent of young people were interested in politics. And that is not all: Among the younger generation of 12 to 25-year-olds, politics has become cool again: 35 percent say that it is "in" to become actively involved.[4]

As much as young people's political activism came as a surprise to the wider public, it has been quietly manifesting itself for some time. As early as 2007, studies among primary school children in Germany showed a high level of self-confidence and a great interest in actively shaping their everyday lives at home and at school. The worries and fears of the six to eleven-year-olds interviewed were also striking: Terrorism and war, increasing poverty, and, in particular, increasing environmental pollution.[5]

The younger generation believes that the *Zeitgeist* is shifting and that Germany is being confronted with a radically different world – and they want to be involved in shaping what comes next. This is a substantial change from previous generations. While protecting the environment or encouraging organic farming was also important to Generation Y, millennials, who are now between 20 and 35 years old, never would have taken to the streets on such a massive scale. Wedged between graduate studies, unpaid or under-paid internships and a succession of temporary contract jobs, many millennials declined to actively participate in political struggles, albeit a little shamefacedly, since "it doesn't help anyway." Faced with the near-collapse of the global financial system in 2007 and the economic crisis that followed, as well as the historically high unemployment rates at the beginning of the 2000s, and now the coronavirus pandemic, they have been occupied with securing their own education in order to find training, work and financial stability.

Generation Y thus became a generation of "ego-tacticians" who were forced to put their own needs first in order to keep their collective heads above water. Many, devoid of the feeling that they had the power to fundamentally change anything, fought quietly in the years before Fridays for Future at school or in the workplace to be able to live and work in ways that aligned with their values. They bought organic products, shared petitions on Facebook and cycled to work while calling for a silent boycott of clothes produced in environmentally harmful or socially exploitative ways. But much of their quiet activism can be categorised as more of a conscious private consumer decision than a political act.[6]

The post-millennial generation, born after 2000, has a different attitude. They see the climate crisis as a truly existential threat, which should propel any thinking politician to action. Individual sacrifice is not enough. They demand greater regulation and fundamental, society-wide change. Their social commitment is anything but quiet and personal; on the contrary, it is explicit, clear and public. If millennials were the ego-tacticians, then Gen Zers are the eco-tacticians. If millennials were quiet, then they are loud. Their demands have echoed throughout the country, Friday after Friday, month after month.

Concerns about the environment and the climate

German youth studies reflect how important issues of environmental pollution and climate change have become for the younger generation, insofar as they continue to climb up the list of issues that "cause fear." In 2002, 62 percent of respondents rated environmental pollution as particularly frightening; by 2019, the figure had risen to 71 percent. Worries about climate change are also trending upwards, currently at 65 percent. All this has pushed other issues into the background. The fear of a terrorist attack is declining, worrying 66 percent of young people, down from 71 percent in 2002. The economy and increasing poverty (52 percent, down from 66 percent), a possible war in Europe (46 percent, down from 59 percent) and the fear of serious illness (48 percent, down from 58 percent) are also losing significance.[7] While the coronavirus pandemic was not yet on the horizon at the time of the 2019 survey, it is likely that economic and health concerns have only increased further since.

For more than ten years, in one youth study after the next, young people have increasingly expressed a growing optimism about their lives – until 2019, when the trend reversed. Even before the onset of the coronavirus pandemic, environmental pollution and the climate crisis started clouding young Germans' perspective on the future. Although 58 percent of 12 to 25-year-olds still believe in their own futures, this number is 3 percent lower than four years ago. In particular, those from well-off families with access to solid educational opportunities have become more sceptical.[8] They are familiar with the research on the climate crisis – and witness to their governments ignoring it. With an expected life expectancy of 90 years or more, they are certain to experience the consequences of global warming themselves.

This concern is the source of their political activism. It is also the main reason for their lack of confidence in the government; less than 3 percent of those who attend FFF demos feel that they can rely on the government to take climate change seriously.[9] They are sharply critical of the politicians in power; at the same time, they continue to believe in democracy. Gen Zers want a radical political turnaround, but they want it to occur within the confines of the existing political system. This is a key difference to the 1960s and 1970s, when a different wave of youth protest swept across Europe. Then, dissatisfaction with the political state of affairs was directed at the ostensibly authoritarian political elite of their parents' and grandparents' generations. Today's eco-tacticians are setting different priorities. They value the democratic structures that make a peaceful and prosperous society possible. They take to the streets not to auger the fall of the system, but to defend a future that they feel is being jeopardised in exchange for short-term electoral gains. Instead of fighting against the generation of their parents and grandparents, they forge alliances with them in order to strengthen their cause.

Many Fridays for Future activists became interested in the movement through Greta Thunberg. Studies show that about one in two young protesters say that she has increased their interest in climate issues, with even higher numbers among young women in Germany.[10]

Luzia is on the FFF organisational committee in Aschaffenburg, a middle-sized city close to Frankfurt am Main. "I'd been politically active for quite a while and had also been to several protests," she says about her involvement before Fridays for Future while refilling her water bottles at one of the large filling stations during the movement's summer convention. "At some point, I realised that everyone here is interested in this, everyone wants to get out on the streets. We can really make a difference now." A total of 1,200 students attended the first Fridays for Future demonstration in her hometown. "Nobody expected it."

Luzia also dreams of a German environmental policy that takes advantage of the country's strong economy to implement a socially just climate policy. "We're all angry and afraid of climate change," says the 16-year-old. Speaking to her, it is easy to imagine how quickly this generation's satisfaction with the democratic system could veer into hostility and dissatisfaction: "If we continue to be ignored, I can see us practicing more civil disobedience and becoming more radical."

"We're not rebelling against our parents," writes Luisa Neubauer, one of FFF's leading figures in Germany, in her book *On the End of the Climate Crisis*, co-authored with Alexander Repenning.

> Instead, we have the feeling that we have to educate our parents – they've become too irresponsible. We need to explain to them that their and our lifestyle is no longer sustainable, and never really was…They need to see that they'll lead us directly into a trap if they don't wake up now.[11]

The dream of most parents to bequeath their children a better world is on the verge of shattering, unless radical changes are implemented quickly. We have arrived in an upside-down world, where the young are the responsible ones who must chastise their elders who are behaving like stubborn children, afraid FFF might take away their gas-guzzling SUVs and all-inclusive trips to Bali.

"How is it possible – despite scientific certainty about the fact that, for decades now, we've been moving in a straight line directly into the greatest catastrophe in human history – that instead of reversing course, we're actually accelerating and moving full speed ahead?" implore Neubauer and Repenning.[12]

To meet the Paris Agreement's 1.5-degree goal, Friday for Future wants the government to end subsidies for fossil fuels, take 25 percent of coal power stations offline immediately, phase out coal-based energy production by 2030 and switch to exclusively renewable energy by 2035. All greenhouse gas emissions must be taxed long-term at a rate of 180 euros per metric ton. Beyond the energy sector, the movement sees a need for greater regulation of housing and construction, industry, transportation and agriculture if global warming is to be limited.

And Fridays for Future is unwilling to concede: "It can't be the sole responsibility of young people to prioritise climate protection. Since politicians hardly acknowledge the need for action, we feel forced to continue fighting until they do,"[13] writes the movement on its webpage.

Climate change as the key issue

Generation Z is growing up at a time in which Western societies are experiencing a "reality shock," writes Sascha Lobo, a journalist. In his book *Reality Shock*, he states, "A new, hyper-complex reality has invaded the previously more or less understandable world." Society may also not have been uncomplicated at end of the twentieth century, but digitalisation and globalisation have linked together what was previously disconnected, made visible what was previously overlooked and destroyed our hope that politicians, business leaders and other elites had a certain control over the course of events.[14]

According to Lobo, there are few major problems left that are not global in scale and digital in nature.

It is precisely this global dimension that makes finding solutions feel so futile, and often leads to resignation. One only needs to look to the United States, the largest global producer of CO_2 emissions, to see how the Trump administration has called the results of decades of climate research into question, instead of attempting to tackle the issue. This resignation is also reflected in the international failure to address numerous other global issues, from the regulation of the internet, economic migration and war, fair trade between the Global North and the Global South to the transition to organic farming.

Climate protests are not a phenomenon limited only to Germany, nor is the climate crisis the only impossible issue that young people have taken upon themselves after older generations have long given up. In a world struggling with huge problems, the momentum for change is increasingly coming from the young generation, who have the optimism to keep on fighting for a better world – and that not only in Germany.

According to a Russian proverb in praise of the country's national poet, "Pushkin is our one and only," and, goes the punchline of a now established political joke, "Putin is our forever." Twenty years after the Kremlin chief took office, this message seems truer than ever. Before Russia's 2018 presidential election, Vladimir Putin's continuation in office seemed like a done deal; no one really believed that a fourth term could be prevented – especially not by facing off in the streets of Moscow against the fearsome special police units (OMON). The notorious OMON was established to fight against terrorists – and protesters. And yet, overnight a generation appeared on the scene that refused to accept the status quo, exactly because it was the only reality it had ever known. Tens of thousands of students, from secondary school to university, suddenly gathered in the streets to demonstrate against the regime. Here too, the protests had never been this young before: While the older generations had long resigned themselves to a life under Vladimir Putin, a life they did not necessarily agree with but which seemed impossible to change, young people had found the will to fight back.

On 14 February 2018, 19-year-old Nikolas Cruz opened fire on students at his former high school in Parkland, Florida, killing 17 people and injuring 17 others before fleeing. He was arrested about an hour later. This was just one of the many mass shootings that happen with horrifying regularity in the United States. No other industrialised country in the world has as many deaths caused by firearms – or such a ubiquitous gun lobby as the National Rifle Association. With Donald Trump's election in 2016, any hope of tightening the country's notoriously lax gun laws seemed to have finally been dashed completely. Here too, students, mostly under 20-year-olds, are the ones trying, despite everything, to break the power of the American gun lobby. The order of events is important here: There is seemingly no chance of success – and yet the young try anyway. And, as with Fridays for Future, those young people are often female. At a demonstration for stricter gun laws, 19-year-old Emma González, a student at the Parkland high school, pointed the finger directly at her elders: "The people in government who are voted into power are lying to us [...] And us kids seem to be the only ones who notice and are prepared to call B.S."[15]

Young people who participate in activism as adolescents are building the skills that will keep them politically agile for life. The major significance of the FFF movement lies in its ability to mobilise so many young people who – through their climate activism – will then become active citizens, writes Mattias Wahlström's research group about the Fridays for Future protests. Political participation as a young person encourages individuals to remain politically engaged throughout their lifetimes.[16] Through its inherent focus on young people, the fight against the climate crisis is thus laying the foundation for a more engaged activism in other political arenas. If you want to reduce CO_2, you will inevitably have to develop new ideas about how we live, eat, travel and stay healthy. Similarly, issues such as the slow digital rollout, inadequate investment in education, the lack of prospects for a secure pension system or the high national debt suddenly also become part and parcel of the larger conversation about a carbon-neutral future. FFF activists have already begun to consider all these issues: Solving the climate crisis is only the beginning.

Job opportunities increase politicisation

More than anything else, shifts in the labour market over that last decade have provided the younger generation with the necessary leeway to engage in political activism. Compared to young people who came of age at the turn of the millennium, the current generation did not have to worry about finding a job once they finished school (until the outbreak of the coronavirus pandemic, that is). Germany is an interesting case study as the economy grew consistently for nearly a decade, leading many companies to recruit young people while they were still in school into their apprenticeship programs. Firms were desperate to find employees – and not only the highly-qualified high achievers; there was a shortage of bakers as well as of doctors, and electricians were as rare as pharmacists. A growing number of apprenticeships remained unfilled.

When a generation is able to look ahead without worry about their professional lives, particularly the well-educated among them have the time and energy to consider larger issues in their societies. Times of economic growth thus become the breeding ground for well-founded criticism of the previous generations' lifestyles and choices. At first glance this state of affairs seems paradoxical: Young people protesting *because* they are doing well and not *despite* that fact? But that is precisely what happens, in large part because youth protests are often fuelled by the middle classes and sustained political protest tends to emerge from positions of privilege. Young people from socially secure homes, usually the better educated ones, can afford to be socially and politically active without risking further education or a professional career.[17]

As Germans rebuilt their country following the Second World War, young people remained largely apolitical; in both German states, young adults were primarily concerned with building up a new life for themselves in the emerging world order. Helmut Schelsky published a pioneering study on this subject, likely the first empirical youth study of the post-war period in Europe, in which he interviewed cohorts born between 1925 and 1940 in West Germany. At the end of the Second World War, Germany was ideologically bankrupt, destroyed by war and economically devastated. Young people who had been brought up within the spirit of National Socialism were suddenly confronted with both the collapse of the regime and denazification. Schelsky called them the "sceptical generation":

> This generation is more critical, sceptical, distrustful and has little faith or at, a minimum, fewer illusions in its social consciousness and self-confidence than all preceding young generations. [It] masters the banality of life as it is presented to them and is proud of it.[18]

In his research, Schelsky vividly demonstrated for the first time how shared collective experiences, in combination with the emergence of new political and cultural constellations, shape many members of the affected age groups in similar ways, reflected in comparable personality traits, emotional attitudes and perspectives on the future. In this case, he was able to demonstrate how oppressive economic conditions led the generation that came into adulthood in the immediate post-war period to develop pragmatic survival strategies – and not a desire for political protest.

The following generation, those born between 1940 and 1955, profited from the German "Wirtschaftswunder," the economic boom of the 1950s, during which economic concerns faded into the background. It was precisely this foundational experience of material security and peace that enabled young people in West Germany to confront social issues, and led to the birth of the 1968 student movement which has remained a benchmark for political commitment and activism in Germany. What becomes clear is that widespread access to economic opportunities makes it more likely for young people to engage in political activism, whereas economic hardship and job insecurity usually prevent them from engaging in political activities and encourage them to focus on ensuring their own livelihoods.

What will happen to Generation Z when the coronavirus pandemic drags them – and the world as a whole – into a major economic downturn? Will high youth unemployment silence this politicised generation by forcing them to reorient toward finding jobs and completing the best degrees possible? Based on what we already know, this seems unlikely. Even if the economy does falter in response to the pandemic, Germany's young generation is already far too politicised and self-confident to retreat from the political arena – unless the coronavirus recession is particularly painful and long-lasting. That being said, independent of the pandemic, larger demographic changes are playing into the hands of Gen Zers, likely buoying at least their economic futures: As in most European countries, German baby boomers are heading for retirement and the chasm they will leave behind is huge. For every 1.4 million baby boomers (born between 1955 and 1970 in Germany; in other countries earlier) retiring per year, only roughly 750,000 young people will enter the job market. The annual birth rate of those following behind them will not even reach that 750,000. In short, significantly more people will retire in the years to come than younger people will be born. What remains to be seen is whether the economic crisis will eliminate more jobs than the mass retirement of the baby boomers will make available.

A new type of movement

Fridays for Future is a new type of movement. Unlike many of its predecessors, including the student movement of the 1960s and 1970s (the so-called "'68ers"), this movement is not making demands for new privileges, greater freedoms or the renewal of a rigid and conservative society. Its ultimate goal is far grander and far more existential: To ensure the survival of humanity through greater restrictions and regulation of key industries and activities. This is a new kind of street protest. While the '68ers revolted against their parents in a battle for new freedoms, today's young generation is fighting – as Luisa Neubauer and Alexander Repenning put it – to educate their parents. It is not about gaining greater personal freedoms but about restricting freedoms that are harmful to the environment and thus to society as a whole. Consumption, energy use, transportation – our society has lived beyond its means for far too long.

There are a few parallels though: Like the '68er movement, FFF has consciously positioned itself outside of the confines of parliamentary politics. While many of its activists are left-leaning and interested in 'green' politics (and some are even members of political parties), the movement itself maintains a clear distance from official partisan politics. Its grassroots organisation is impressive, and the fact that most of its leadership positions are held by women is remarkable, unlike the 1968ers, whose movement was led by men. The movement's heroes were men like Rudi Dutschke, a provocative and talented student leader; they were dominant figures at demonstrations and on university campuses and made no secret about their role as political leaders.

Fridays for Future has adopted a different style and employs completely different forms of protest. The movement is inspired more by twentieth-century Pride marches than by street fighting. Their demonstrations are akin to street festivals, with music and dancing. There are no leaders who predominate; instead, several notably eloquent speakers, who attach more importance to being recognised as members of the group, share the spotlight. Those who seek the spotlight too much are quickly reined in by their peers. This form of protest makes it difficult for opponents to attack. Those who play the role of agitators or try to stir things up appear ridiculous in the face of good-humoured crowds of demonstrators. The protests make clear that political action is directly linked to everyday life, and that everyday life is directly connected to politics – like that to-go coffee in a plastic cup.

Political action based on facts

After the end of the protest at the Saturn electronics store, the activists march towards Dortmund's main railway station. They continue to chant various slogans, including calling for climate justice and a ban on disposable coffee cups or SUVs, until they board commuter train line 2, which will bring them back to their camp at the summer convention. On the park grounds, small groups of young people move back and forth between the kitchen tent, the awareness point and conference areas, with colourful arrows showing them the way. A small queue forms in front of the kiosk tent around noon, as people stand in line to buy fair trade lemonade and vegan muesli bars. The hillside park looks idyllic in the summer sun. This is Fridays for Future pausing for a moment of self-reflection, before moving on with renewed energy to save the environment.

In the afternoon, the area around the kitchen tent slowly empties as activists meet for workshops; along with everyone else, Catriona and Nora head to the Schiller Secondary School, where the classrooms have been turned into seminar rooms. There is hardly a journalist who has missed an opportunity to set up the punch line that Fridays for Future protesters have been skipping school on Fridays since the beginning of 2019 but voluntarily spend the summer holidays in class. But for the activists, this is no joke. They have come to Dortmund to learn about and better understand climate change. At a time when public debates are becoming increasingly heated, when fake news and "perceived truths" are ever-present, these environmentally conscious students are focused on facts. That alone is a huge statement.

The workshops are less concerned with the future of the movement than with topics such as "Digitalisation and the energy revolution," "the sustainability crisis beyond the climate crisis" or "changing the education system." And they really get down to the bare bones with "meat – the climate killer." Apart from information on the climate and sustainability issues, many workshops provide tangible skills related to activist work: "public speaking" or "creative political action." All in all, the schedule fills two large, tightly printed poster boards. Catriona and Nora hesitate a little in front of one of the boards at the entrance to the secondary school. The two 16-year-olds would like to attend several workshops – one on feminism in social movements, for example – but many are scheduled at the same time. In the end, they decide to go for "my t-shirt and melting polar ice caps?!" and "meat – the climate killer" after that.

Gen Zers trust science just as much as they mistrust party politics. In polls taken during Fridays for Future protests, five out of six activists said that science could help solve environmental problems.[19] Their interest in politics stems from their interest in the issues – first and foremost, issues that affect them emotionally, especially environmental protection and climate change. After the recent wave of hot summers, this generation feels they have been given a taste of the consequences of the climate crisis. They fear for their existence and are not afraid to call out those they deem responsible: After all, the German government committed itself to the goals of the Paris Climate Agreement, but then did far too little to ensure the benchmarks contained therein were met.

This is why Generation Z is taking a stand. At the climate camp in Dortmund, it becomes clear how all-encompassing the vision behind Fridays for Future's fight against global warming actually is. In workshop room 8A, named after the geneticist Barbara McClintock, Constantin has arranged the chairs into a circle. As the participants, significantly more young women than young men, drift in, the 18-year-old quickly sets up the projector. Constantin has just graduated from secondary school, but his activism on the issue of fast fashion dates back to 2016, when Primark, a discount clothing chain, opened a store in his hometown. The secondary school student first did research online and later travelled all over Germany to talk to experts about the lack of sustainability and poor working conditions in the clothing industry. He presented the results of his research at a project day in his school.

"On average, a T-shirt travels between 18,000 and 50,000 kilometres during the course of its production," he says to the workshop participants. "The garment industry is the second largest polluter in the world." He then asks the participants to line up in the order in which they bought their last piece of clothing. They converse animatedly among themselves as they slowly find their spots. At the end of the row, among the most recent purchases, the conversation goes on the longest, but then they also quiet down. "You've bought a piece of clothing since Monday?" Constantin asks the participant on the farthest end, briefly registering a moment of surprise. But without judging, he moves on, "online or at a store?"

The differing responses to Constantin's exercise show just how much the personal consequences of their activism vary between the participants. Some attach great importance to fair trade and organic labels, others choose to wear second-hand fashion. Many are vegetarian or vegan, and want to apply this ethos to their clothing as well. After all, "Environmental protection is only available in vegan" is one of the slogans that can be read over and over again at FFF protests.

As Constantin works his way down the row of participants, the names of major fashion brands – all of which have been criticised for their labour conditions – are mentioned repeatedly. Everyone at the workshop came to learn more about ethical behaviour, but also about the fundamental problems within the industry. No one came here to lord their moral superiority as a critical customer over the others or to have their ethical behaviour applauded. Still, few can keep up with Klara when it comes to sustainability: Her black top was worn by her grandmother as a young girl.

The workshop lasts about two hours, accompanied by a stream of lively but focused discussion. Looking around the room, it is striking how much the activists resemble each other. Most of the participants in the workshop are white; people of colour and those with a family history of migration are in the minority – even though one in three members of this generation has a parent or grandparent who was not born in Germany. Most activists come from schools that prepare them to attend university; students from more vocationally oriented schools are rare. Under these circumstances, can Fridays for Future really influence and speak for an entire generation?

Notes

1 Neubauer and Repenning 2019, p. 73.
2 DeMoor et al. 2020.
3 Neubauer 2020.
4 Schneekloth and Albert 2019, p. 63.
5 Andresen et al. 2017.
6 Hurrelmann and Albrecht 2014.
7 Schneekloth and Albert 2019, p. 56.
8 Schneekloth and Albert 2019, p. 183.
9 Haunss et al. 2019.
10 Haunss et al. 2019.
11 Neubauer and Repenning 2019, p. 33.
12 Neubauer and Repenning 2019, p. 15.
13 Fridays for Future Deutschland 2021.
14 Lobo 2019, p. 10.
15 https://www.nytimes.com/2018/02/18/us/emma-gonzalez-florida-shooting.html
16 Wahlström et al. 2019.
17 Hurrelmann and Quenzel 2013.
18 Schelsky 1963, p. 381.
19 Haunss et al. 2019, p. 78.

Chapter 2

Greta's generation
The face of Gen Z?

The face of the climate movement

"Greta's coming!" Despite the school holidays, about 2,000 people have come to the Fridays for Future (FFF) protest in Berlin's Invalidenpark. They start call and response chants, dance and hold up banners with pithy slogans. On stage, the speakers rotate in quick succession. When one of the speakers – a 13-year-old student – gets tongue-tied, it simply underlines how eloquently each of them is able to get their message across with heart and determination.

But those who came exclusively for Greta Thunberg will be disappointed. The Swedish climate activist speaks only briefly, towards the end of the event. On stage, she appears almost childlike, much smaller than the rest of the young people around here, despite her 16 years. She speaks freely, confidently, but somewhat flatly and matter of fact. She speaks in English. At the end, she begins a call and response herself; it seems as if she has left her comfort zone – and is a little proud of it.

This young Swedish girl is the face of the global climate movement. At the World Economic Forum in Davos, Switzerland, she flung a "I want you to panic!" at the entire gathering of global business elites. She has spoken at the Climate Change Conference in Katowice, the United Nations in New York and the EU Parliament in Strasbourg. The trip to New York took her two weeks: Thunberg travelled by racing yacht (a yacht in name only, since it had neither toilet facilities nor proper beds) to avoid unnecessary CO_2 emissions. The return journey by catamaran to the World Climate Conference in Madrid in December 2019 lasted another three weeks. During the initial phase of the pandemic in the first half of 2020, she withdrew to her parents' apartment and communicated only via digital media.

Without Greta Thunberg's singular action, no student would have thought to demonstrate for climate action on Fridays – and at a time when school is normally in session. And yet, here in Berlin's Invalidenpark, Thunberg speaks for only five minutes. No trace of the "Greta cult." Greta is one of many who will speak on that day.

Fridays for Future believes in itself as a grassroots movement. On the whole, this seems to be the case, but within the German movement in particular, there is some criticism that a small leadership clique has formed that wields too much influence. The approximately 600 local groups work independently, with weekly telephone conferences between them to coordinate the work nationwide.

Asked about Greta Thunberg, a young Fridays for Future activist spontaneously blurts out, "That's just this personality cult thing, isn't it?" Then he briefly ponders the question again, before adding,

> I don't think it's bad if Fridays for Future has some kind of representative with Greta, but she's just the one who started it, she's not the whole movement. Her opinions should not be considered representative of all of us.

Can we actually consider Generation Z a "Generation Greta?" Possibly, but members of this generation would likely disagree. They believe themselves to be far too individualistic to gather unconditionally behind a single leading figure. Within the movement, attitudes towards Greta Thunberg are often ambivalent; outside of the movement, in some school classes, the name Greta makes people groan – even though climate protection is important to them. It is frustrating how 'Greta' reduces an entire generation to a single person, says 17-year-old Paul, who is one year away from graduating from Sophie Scholl School in Berlin.

And yet: Greta Thunberg has become the stand-in for the entire movement. As the movement's singular instigator, it is impossible for either activists or the rest of the younger generation to downplay her contribution. An international comparative study of the various protest movements in September 2019 found that, in the 19 cities in 15 different countries included in the survey, an average of 50 percent of respondents said that Greta Thunberg had sparked their interest in the issue of climate change. The motivation to take part in a demonstration or a strike was thus also linked to her person to almost the same extent. This Greta effect is significantly higher among younger than among older age groups.

Movements like Fridays for Future are the fabric from which generations are woven. They never reach all segments of the population, but that is rarely necessary to initiate change. Even during the powerful student protests of the 1960s, it was not "young people" that took to the streets. On the contrary, the activism of 10 percent of the student body was enough to permanently transform entire societies.

Without Greta Thunberg, the Fridays for Future movement for climate action would not exist. She gave the movement its name, she is the reason why, for the first time in recent history, pupils are playing an influential role in public discourse. The fact that, in August 2018, a 15-year-old girl could launch a political movement with such a near-instantaneous global impact says a lot about her generation, especially since in the time after starting her Skolstrejk för klimatet, she has not lost any of her moral authority – which is significantly longer than some European political party leaders manage to keep theirs.

Environmental protection and climate policy have been vitally important for the majority of young people for quite some time. The difference now is that Greta Thunberg has forced her generation to develop an opinion on climate policy writ large and the Fridays for Future protests in particular – whether they support the movement or not. In so doing, she has shaped large parts of her generation into a "Generation Greta."

The concept of a generation

The concept of generations has been discussed in the social sciences since the 1920s, when it was developed by Karl Mannheim, a sociologist and philosopher. He hypothesised that individuals who grow up in a specific time period are shaped by the conditions of their society during their youth to such an extent that they develop a significant number of common values, attitudes and behavioural patterns.[1] This effect is particularly evident in people who grow up in times of crisis.

Mannheim's theory was heavily influenced by the First World War, which had a lasting impact on many young men in that era – although Mannheim ignored its impact on young women wholesale. Although the War was a particularly devastating crisis, other far-reaching technical, political, economic and cultural events or developments can also leave their mark on a generation. The study by Helmut Schelsky mentioned in Chapter 1, which focused on young people in West Germany after the Second World War, was the first empirical study based on this approach.

Since then, a number of generation studies have been conducted, although the term must be used with care. It has still not been empirically proven that values, attitudes and behavioural patterns acquired during adolescence are retained throughout one's lifetime. Several analyses indicate that although young people are clearly influenced by their living conditions, these influences always reflect very general contemporary historical effects that also apply – to a lesser or greater extent – to all other age groups as well. In addition, the term is often used in a superficial way: Marketing experts and journalists on a deadline are quick to proclaim a "Generation Shoulder Bag" or "Generation Maybe" to reflect fashion trends or new consumer habits, in ways that have nothing to do with Karl Mannheim's differentiated concept of a generation.

In this book, we use a concept of 'generation' based on sociological research on the processes of socialisation. According to this concept, the development of an individual's personality is understood as a constant productive processing of internal and external reality – of their physical and psychological disposition on the one hand, and their social and environmental living conditions on the other.[2] This active exploration and intense work on one's own personality reaches its peak in adolescence. After puberty, people reflect on their own lives with increased sensitivity and begin to see themselves through the eyes of others. What individuals experience during this phase – historical events, as well as their political, economic, cultural and technical circumstances – often establishes characteristic, and surprisingly similar, personality patterns across communities.[3]

Greta Thunberg hit a nerve with her independent protest, and large segments of today's young generation were subsequently influenced by her. Without being able to tap into an already widespread feeling of stagnation about the state of climate policy across the globe, her initiative could never have become what it is today. The environmental movement Fridays for Future is based on the work of countless older people, many of whom have been committed to climate protection and an environmentally responsible lifestyle for decades. Without young people's existential fear of climate change, which has been smouldering for some time, Thunberg's message would not have been as effective and its spread not nearly as fast.

The post-war generations

It is virtually impossible to specify when one generation ends and another one begins, as political, economic, cultural and technical factors are always moving at different speeds. We follow a widespread tradition within generation research and use a period of 15 years for each generation. Applying this approach, the following generations can be identified in Germany for the period following the Second World War (the dates and points of emphasis differ in other countries):

- The post-war generation, born between 1925 and 1940 and raised in times of economic hardship and political despair, described as the "sceptical generation."
- The highly politicised "1968ers," born between 1941 and 1955, who grew up during the economic recovery and aggressively confronted the authoritarian legacy of their parents.
- The baby boomers, born between 1956 and 1970, who grew up in a stable welfare economy with a well-functioning democratic system and who today control the levers of power in Germany.
- Generation X, born between 1971 and 1985, who came of age in economically and politically uncertain times.
- Generation Y, born between 1986 and 2000, who grew up as "digital natives" amid enduring economic and political crises such as the 2001 terrorist attack on New York and the Pentagon, the financial crisis in 2008 and the nuclear meltdown in Fukushima in 2011.
- The generation born after 2000, growing up under relatively stable economic circumstances and (until the pandemic hit) with a much better outlook for their financial and personal futures compared to Generation X and Generation Y. This book is about them.

Most authors refer to this last post-war generation in alphabetical order as "Generation Z."[4] The letter Z, however, is neither a metaphor nor does it reflect any concrete demographic or historical realities. Previous generational labels were metaphorical or symbolic ("sceptics" for the rational post-war youth, "X" for an enigmatic generation, "Y" for the probing and ego-tactical search for meaning, the *why*) or era-specific ("baby boomers" for the members of the largest age group, "1968ers" for the student protesters of 1968). Strictly speaking, the fact that the youngest generation has thus far been lazily labelled with the next letter in the alphabet does not fit the established pattern.

Nevertheless, this terminology has become firmly established in both empirical research and political life, and we will follow the same practice. Despite the ostensible uniformity in naming this generation, Gen Z is deeply fragmented. On the one hand, parts of this generation can be called "Generation Greta" with good reason, as the activist has become a symbol of the exceptional political commitment demonstrated by the opinion-leading groups within their ranks. On the other hand, certain segments of this generation will be severely affected by the economic recession caused by the coronavirus pandemic and can symbolically be termed "Generation Covid" – an especially tidy designation, since so many of those who will suffer the toughest consequences were 19 when the pandemic hit.

Who is Greta Thunberg?

In May 2018, a 15-year-old girl wins a writing competition on environmental issues sponsored by the *Svenska Dagbladet*. After the Swedish daily newspaper publishes her essay, she is contacted by environmental activists. Together, they devise a plan on how she could become politically active, with the budding activist taking a special interest in the idea of school strikes, an idea first developed by students at a high school in Parkland, Florida. Following a deadly rampage at their school in February 2018, they campaigned for stricter gun control laws in the United States with public "strikes."

After trying unsuccessfully for weeks to find others to join her, she decides to stage a solo strike in front of the Swedish parliament in Stockholm.[5] She places a plywood board next to her with the message "school strike for the climate" and remains there for hours. She returns week after week. After a while, public and media interest in the shy, unassuming girl begins to grow. She gives more and more interviews; her answers are concise and well-formulated. The public attention also helps her to slowly overcome her isolation and reluctance to make social contact.

Greta is not a typical representative of her generation – and not only because of the media attention bestowed upon her. As a youngster, she was diagnosed with Asperger syndrome, OCD and selective mutism and attributes her activism directly to that. "That basically means that I only speak when I think it's necessary," she writes. "Now is one of those moments."[6] She says that "I have Aspberger's syndrome, and to me, almost everything is black or white," which is why she does not understand how people can simply carry on as before despite a climate crisis that threatens their very existence. "If the emissions have to stop, then we must stop the emissions. To me, that is black or white. There are no grey areas when it comes to survival. Either we go on as a civilisation or we don't."[7]

"People say that since I have Asperger I couldn't possibly have put myself in this position," writes Greta Thunberg.

> But that's exactly why I did this. Because if I would have been 'normal' and social I would have organised myself in an organisation, or started an organisation by myself. But since I am not that good at socialising I did this instead.[8]

By "this," she of course means her solitary school strike.

Greta, an icon of the environmental movement

As extraordinary as Greta Thunberg's life story may seem, in many ways it is typical for her age group – which is precisely why her protest, her line of argumentation and her view of the world have resounded so widely among young people, turning many of them into a "Generation Greta."

(Generation) Greta knows the facts

She did not begin her strike on a whim. At a time when political leaders such as Donald Trump in the United States, Jair Bolsonaro in Brazil or the Brexiteers in Great Britain operate with "alternative facts," or defy experts, and major powers like China and Russia engage in targeted disinformation, she relies on the findings of leading scientists and considers their results factually undeniable. Her activism began after researching the issue for an essay – only then did indignation follow.

Greta Thunberg has set an example with her fact-based activism. Travelling through a country like Germany and talking to young people about climate change today means finding sound expertise everywhere. 13-year-old Adrian from Berlin demands that climate change should be addressed more intensively at school. There is currently too much disinformation, he says. In Ludwigsburg, a small city close to Stuttgart, a 16-year-old argues that 70 percent of industrial CO_2 emissions are caused by only 120 companies. It is this emphasis on the facts that makes FFF protests so effective.

(Generation) Greta measures politicians by the commitments they make

As part of the Paris Climate Agreement, 197 signatory countries pledged to reduce their CO_2 emissions to meet a 1.5-degree target. By September 2019, only two countries had adopted appropriate national climate action plans: Morocco and Gambia. Among the five doing enough to limit global warming to two degrees, there is not a single Western, industrialised nation. This state of affairs is precisely what Fridays for Future is attempting to change with their protests.

At the World Economic Forum in Davos, Switzerland, in January 2019, Greta Thunberg implored the assembled political and business elites, "I want you to act as if the house is on fire, because it is." The climate crisis threatens our civilisation. Everyone who understands this, she said, must raise their voice. Then, she uttered the line that she will forever be remembered for: "I want you to panic."[9]

(Generation) Greta feels they are victims of misguided climate policies

Thunberg's fundamental message is that politicians must take action immediately, since her generation must live on this planet much longer than they will. Those who continue to hold on to the status quo are gambling with the future of not only the current generation but those to come. "We are young, we are here, we want a future without fear!" was, roughly translated, the chant heard at FFF protests across Germany on Fridays, until the pandemic hit. In its German version, it refers explicitly to the future being stolen from them.

Greta's generation is driven by the concern that the world will no longer be worth inhabiting in just a few short years. "Solving the climate crisis is the greatest and most complex challenge Homo sapiens have ever faced. The main solution, however, is so simple that even a small child can understand it," Thunberg believes. "We have to stop our emissions of greenhouse gases."[10]

(Generation) Greta tries to close ranks between the generations

Although Greta and her generation argue that politicians are currently gambling away the future of her generation, their position does not automatically culminate in confrontation, but in a request for concrete action: "We are begging you for help," Greta said on her visit to Berlin – a recurring motif in many of her speeches, as is the plea for an alliance with parents and grandparents. The relationship between parents and children has never been as harmonious as it is today. When students and young people take to the streets, they are protesting against a system that produces ever more greenhouse gases; they are not protesting against their parents. While Greta Thunberg's parents actively support her activism, parents in Germany write excuse notes for their children to hand in at school, so they can attend climate demonstrations without getting into trouble for skipping class.

(Generation) Greta is a generation of strong women

A clear majority of the participants at FFF demonstrations are female. Luisa Neubauer and Carla Reemtsma are two of the familiar faces among the many women and girls who attend the German protests. While this might seem surprising at first, since young women previously expressed less interest in and commitment to politics than young men, the climate crisis has changed that. Climate change is of particular interest to girls and young women, and more and more of them are entering the public arena to speak out on behalf of the environment. They are also at the forefront of other issues – be it Emma González in her fight against the US weapons lobby or sea captain Carola Rackete, whose ship is engaged in rescuing stranded refugees in the Mediterranean.

The growing interest of young women in political issues has been evident for 15 years. German youth studies show that, since 2002, the willingness of young people to become politically active has steadily increased and a closer look reveals that this is due in large part to the growing interest among women and girls. Their numbers continue to increase, and currently their interest slightly exceeds that of young men. In 2002, 57 percent of 12 to 25-year-old women and girls described political engagement as "not important," whereas today this figure has fallen to 38 percent. In contrast, the number of female respondents who considered an interest in politics to be important or somewhat important rose from 31 to 59 percent.[11]

This interest has been further boosted by the rise in environmental activism, as the issue of climate change seems to speak more to girls and women than to boys and men, perhaps because of its existential and all-encompassing threat to humanity.

Greta Thunberg represents that part of the younger generation that is already setting the tone in public. She thus stands for her entire generation.

Notes

1　Mannheim 1970.
2　Hurrelmann and Bauer 2018.
3　Hurrelmann and Quenzel 2019.
4　Seemiller and Grace 2017.
5　Thunberg 2019, p. 50.
6　Thunberg 2019, p. 30.
7　Thunberg 2019, p. 21.
8　Thunberg 2019, p. 47.
9　Thunberg 2019, p. 39.
10　Thunberg 2019, p. 36.
11　Schneekloth and Albert 2019, p. 52.

Chapter 3

Solidarity versus intergenerational conflict

How Gen Z are engaging society

Brexit – a symbol for intergenerational conflict

Wearing a black and blue chequered shirt and tight black jeans, Jack is drinking a cup of tea in his spacious kitchen in Wedding, an up-and-coming district of Berlin, the warm evening air gently wafting through an open window. Like many 25-year-olds, he takes his tea in the classic British hipster way – with oat milk. Jack moved to Germany with his girlfriend Rosie in 2017. Since then, he has learned German and found not only a job as a project manager with a logistics company, but also a flat in the capital city's overheated rental market.

"Those are Rosie's books over there," says Jack, pointing to several stacks in a corner of the living room. "I guess we'll need another shelf." The young Brit still sounds a little surprised that he has finally made a home for himself in Berlin. For the first time, they are not living in a short-term let but have their own lease and are settling in for the long haul.

For Jack and Rosie, life in Berlin-Wedding is also a conscious farewell to the United Kingdom: The ongoing social dynamics kicked up in the wake of the Brexit debacle were a conflict they simply could not resolve. As Brexit dragged on, important issues, including the ailing NHS, continued to be ignored while British policy remained hopelessly entangled in the chaos of Britain's withdrawal from the EU. Nowhere in Europe more than in Britain are the societal consequences of this failure to find an intergenerational consensus more evident.

Jack saw all this coming. During the Brexit referendum, he fought for Britain to remain in the European Union, coordinating pro-EU volunteers in Canterbury in southeast England and going door to door to campaign for the European Union and warn against the dire consequences of withdrawal. His studies were secondary. He worked on his thesis in his off-hours, often at night – Britain's EU membership was too important.

In the end, it was overwhelmingly older voters who refused to listen to his arguments. When 51.9 percent voted to leave the EU on 23 June 2016, Jack wondered whether this Britain was still his home. "That was the point when we thought, 'We don't want to live here,'" he recalls today. "'We have to leave now because time is running out.'"

The Brexit referendum has radically altered the debate about Europe, in particular as young people have come to realise just how weak their position is in today's ageing societies. Roughly 70 percent of 18 to 24-year-olds voted against Brexit. They did not stand a chance against the older generation: 60 percent of over-65-year-olds ultimately decided the referendum by voting for the "leave" campaign. Although commentators criticised younger voters for their lower turnout at the polls, they were simply demographically outnumbered by the cohort of 65-and-overs in the United Kingdom.

Beyond its political and economic ramifications, Brexit was also a symbol of the societal wounds caused by a brewing intergenerational conflict. "Deep down, I had this vague anger against the generations before me," Jack recalls, "against the generation of my parents and the baby boomers." Indeed, Brexit's consequences will be borne primarily by the younger generation: Even before the details of Brexit were clear, several major companies announced plans to relocate their production sites to countries in the European Union, and British companies are already selling fewer goods to continental Europe. All this means fewer jobs in Britain, affecting especially those who are now entering the labour market for the first time. For them, Brexit also makes it more difficult to work in the EU, should jobs dry up in Britain – which is why Jack and Rosie did not think twice before quickly moving to Berlin.

Austerity at the expense of a younger generation

Political divides have always been deeper in the UK than in Germany. The first-past-the-post voting system favours not only a clear balance of power, but also electoral clientelism. As a rule, the dividing line runs between wealthy rural areas, which vote conservatively (especially in the south of England), and poorer Labour strongholds in the now deindustrialised north.

In recent years, however, a further rift has developed within British political life – that between young and old. Boris Johnson became prime minister after the 2019 parliamentary elections on a wave of support from those 65 and older, among whom Johnson's Conservative Party enjoyed a 47-point lead. On the other end of the demographic spectrum, Labour led with 43 points and a solid majority of young votes. According to pollster Ipsos MORI, "age continues to be a key dividing line, and in fact the age divide has increased even further since 2017."[1]

Jack is no exception to this pattern. In the UK, he was a member of Woodcraft Folk, a left-wing educational movement for children and young people; in Berlin, he joined the German counterpart of the socialist Falcon Youth.

Euro-scepticism has a long tradition in the United Kingdom. Nonetheless, without the 2008 financial crisis, the idea of a British exit from the EU would have never gained a foothold. The financial collapse plunged the UK, with its outsized banking sector, into a deep recession and left a gaping hole in the revenues of the national treasury. As the budget deficit climbed to over 10 percent of economic output, the Conservative-led coalition government implemented a rigorous austerity plan, cutting spending across all government sectors. This austerity accompanied Jack throughout his youth. In particular, the past decade's massive cutbacks affected social groups who did not vote for the Tories – including communities in the poorer north and the young.

When Jack thinks of austerity, the first thing that comes to mind is the Educational Maintenance Allowance for students from poor families: £15 a week for personal use. When the Tory government abolished this allowance, it meant that many of his friends could no longer afford the bus ride to the city centre to spend a Sunday with him. Around the same time, the government also tripled tuition fees from £3,000 to £9,000 per year. Jack's cohort was the first to pay. As a result, he left university £47,000 in debt; his older brother had paid a little less than a fifth of that.

"These are the things that affected me directly," says Jack. "But similar things happened everywhere. My parents' generation could buy a house in London for just £70,000." Today, alongside London's expansion into a global financial behemoth, properties in the British capital are among the most expensive in the world. At the same time, older generations are buying rental apartments as an investment for their retirement. While "buy-to-let" schemes have been heavily criticised for pushing up real estate prices, making it more difficult for first-time buyers to purchase property, Jack's generation is even further down the ladder – nicknamed "Generation Rent," the generation of tenants.

"Brexit was the icing on the cake of six years of austerity," says Jack. "I really felt that the generations before us enjoyed all the privileges and they were now pulling up the ladder behind them. A terrible feeling."

Between pension and education

While the United Kingdom is trapped in a constant struggle over Brexit and its aftermath, Germany has experienced one of the longest booms in its history – at least until the coronavirus pandemic put an abrupt end to it in March 2020. The country experienced record employment; youth unemployment was at an all-time low. Although social inequality has increased over the past 20 years, the gap between rich and poor is by no means as wide as in the United Kingdom.

However, Germany has a much more serious demographic problem, as it faces a future with one of the oldest populations in the world. In terms of sheer numbers, older generations can easily outvote younger ones: There are 22 million people between the ages of 18 and 40, compared to 48 million people over 40. The population under the age of 18 stands at 13 million.

More and more, these young people become aware that this demographic imbalance puts a huge burden of pensions on their shoulders. Pension policy is only one example among many that – in Germany, as elsewhere – has undermined confidence in the government and its willingness to take future needs into account among the younger generation. While politicians have ruled out an increase in the retirement age to balance the public pension fund, younger generations entertain few illusions about their own futures: 85 percent of 17 to 27-year-old Germans expect they will have to work well beyond the current retirement age of 67. Sixty-eight percent are worried about the small size of their eventual pensions and thus about poverty in old age. Given the current state of legislation, this scenario is absolutely realistic. Even those employed at a full salary without interruption after graduation can, unlike their parents and grandparents, at best expect to receive 45 percent of their final salary as a pension.[2]

Generation Z is well aware of the fact that the public pension system has been so decimated since 2000 that it will no longer provide enough to live on by the time they retire. Employer pension top-up incentives or private pension plans seem either too complicated or insufficient. And, in the end, most of them do not have money left over at the end of the month to invest in provisions for their old age. Even among those who can afford it, saving money for retirement seems increasingly hopeless, because they do not believe they will be able to fall back on those amounts in 40 or 50 years. To add insult to injury, the state's ability to compensate for lower pensions is likely to remain compromised for many years to come by the huge fiscal response programmes instituted in the wake of the coronavirus pandemic. As a result, members of the younger generation feel neglected by society and the state, compared to older demographics: 84 percent are convinced that the state could still ensure a good pension for them if it really wanted to.[3]

In any case, the decisions surrounding the future of old-age provisions will certainly not lie with the young generation. In terms of numbers, young people are not a particularly important voter group. German political parties only become interested in voters as they approach 50, which is one of the many reasons why politicians in Germany prefer discussing pensions or the nursing care crisis to tackling education or the lack of available day-care spots.

Meanwhile, the ability of the younger generation to establish a sustainable life for themselves based on their own hard work has decreased proportionately to the rising property prices over the last 20 years. Economist Thomas Piketty analysed data from 20 countries over several centuries and concluded: Older generations laid the foundation for their wealth during an economic period that is, historically speaking, almost an anomaly. During this period, incomes in European social market economies increased faster than returns on capital investments. Today, however, the situation is the other way around: Capital investments generate far greater profits than people can feasibly earn from their labour.[4]

As a result, while many high earners from the 1968er and baby boomer generation (who are now over 50) were able to finance a house or flat through their own labour, today, even young people from the upper middle class are dependent on "the bank of mom and dad" to get on the housing ladder.

In this context, journalist Julia Friedrichs refers to an "inheritance society." According to her calculations, in Germany, 250 billion euros are transferred to the next generation every year: "A transfer of assets never seen before." However, this image of Germany as a society of heirs only applies to half of the population. Ninety-nine percent of assets are in the hands of the more affluent half of German society, while the poorer half owns just 1 percent. "Inheritances pass this inequality onto the next generation," Friedrichs concludes.[5]

Belonging to one generation versus another is thus also a question of social justice. Young people are more often in fixed-term contracts than older individuals; long-term financial planning thus becomes difficult, and thus also the purchase of property.

The Foundation for the Rights of Future Generations in Germany argues that this lack of solidarity between generations is damaging for society, calling for a reform of the inheritance tax. "If the existing, excessive tax exemptions alone were struck down, it would generate around eight billion euros in additional revenue. This money could finance an 'intergenerational solidarity fund.'"[6]

Without such intergenerational solidarity measures, the majority of the younger generation might soon believe that the older generations really are – in Jack's words – "pulling the ladder up" behind them.

An intergenerational conflict over climate change?

It is ten to eight in the morning at a secondary school in Giessen, less than 100 kilometres north of Frankfurt am Main. Outside, the grey courtyard is still dark. Inside, a class of ninth graders is sitting in a circle in the media library surrounded by books, newspapers and computer workstations, discussing what characterises their generation. Among the students of class 9c, one finds Leon dressed in a green hoodie. He is interested in politics but found Greta Thunberg's speech at the United Nations "embarrassing." A few chairs away is Emil, a passionate skateboarder, who wonders why so many older people are making political decisions for young people. Finally, there is Pia, sitting on the other side of the circle, who works with refugees in her spare time.

As different as these students may be, one topic is important to all of them: environmentalism and the climate crisis. Irrespective of their individual feelings about Greta Thunberg, almost all of them have been to a Fridays for Future protest on the Berliner Platz square here in Giessen.

"The protests don't really help," Leon says. "But you feel a little better about yourself and have the feeling you're taking some responsibility for these issues." A classmate objects, "I think Fridays for Future has put pressure on politicians." After all, everyone's aware of the protests, he explains. "The Greens got more votes in the last election," Lukas agrees. "And that has something to do with Fridays for Future."

Clearly, the climate crisis has the potential to spark a major intergenerational conflict today. Gen Zers did not start the fight against fossil fuels; on the contrary, the Green Party, a political party committed to the responsible use of our planet's resources, have been elected to the German parliament, the Bundestag, since 1983.

However, Fridays for Future has managed to place the fight against climate change at the top of the political agenda. The protests have increased public awareness by successfully reframing the issue as an intergenerational conflict instead of simply a political and ideological question. Until recently, climate policy was a question of priorities. While it was central to the Green Party platform, the conservative Christian Democratic Union (CDU) and the pro-business Liberals (FDP) remained more concerned with protecting economic interests, while the

Social Democratic Party of Germany (SPD) and the Left Party (Die Linke) put their emphasis on workers' interests.

Fridays for Future has successfully challenged this framing: Climate issues are not a question of left versus right or employers versus employees, the movement argues, but rather about young versus old. Because climate issues are issues to be faced in the future, they should not be subject to existing, outdated, ideologies or world views. Instead, politicians should focus on the protection of the interests – and existence – of younger generations.

The dangers of global warming have been widely known since the 1980s – but in fact, since then, humanity has pumped more CO_2 into the atmosphere than in all of history together, as the two German FFF activists Luisa Neubauer and Alexander Repenning write. For both of them, it is obvious who is to blame. They want to hold older generations "collectively responsible" for their actions. "Responsible for leaving us a natural environment in shambles. Responsible for not acting when there was plenty of time."[7]

"We are growing up in a world in which climate chaos is becoming the norm," Neubauer said at the annual general meeting of the energy supplier RWE. Her generation's future will be overshadowed by the collapse of many global ecosystems.[8]

Unsurprisingly, the Greens are the party that has most benefited from the climate movement. This is true for Germany, as for other European countries. Only during the initial phase of the coronavirus pandemic did the party briefly lose support in opinion polls as support for the governing parties surged. But local elections in France in late June 2020 have already shown how much power the FFF movement has channelled to the Green parties. The movement has the most public credibility in addressing the issue of climate change. And the sooner the coronavirus crisis is contained, the greater its influence will be.

Alliances instead of conflict

Back at the secondary school in Giessen. Despite all the problems, nobody here wants to start an intergenerational conflict. "Well, I don't blame my parents and grandparents," says one student. "They knew that CO_2 wasn't good for the climate, but they didn't realise the extent of it." "That wouldn't help," says Jolina. "We can't go back in time and change the past." And Leon says, "My parents' generation did not have the opportunity to save energy either. The light bulbs they had back then, they were energy hogs."

Listening to the students, you could begin to imagine that their parents had not grown up in the 1990s, but shortly after the Second World War. Energy-saving light bulbs and refrigerators – these were only available much more recently, says Leon. Without these, his parents and their generation had tried to make the best of it, but could only make it so far.

No one in 9c is in favour of an intergenerational conflict. Despite all this sympathy with the past, their demands for the present remain clear: "But I'd still like my grandparents to try and do a little more," says one student, speaking for many. "They can still try to change things now."

Instead of fighting the generation of their parents and grandparents, Gen Z is instead trying to enlist them in their struggle. Instead of blaming the older generation for not tackling climate change when there was still time, they attribute fault to "the" politicians, especially those in the governing parties, the Social Democrats and the Christian Democrats.

In large part, young people defend their parents because they get along with them better than any previous generation. A deep understanding runs between Gen Zers and their parents, and together they work to shape their everyday lives. According to studies of young people in Germany, 42 percent get on very well with their parents and another 50 percent say that they get along well despite occasional disagreements. This consensus has steadily increased over the past 15 years. Generation Z and their parents trust each other; parents serve as role models; their children respect their achievements.[9]

Generation Z values their parents as their most important advisers and supporters, while simultaneously trying to convince them to change their environmental behaviour. They take their parents seriously, but also want to be taken seriously by their parents. In short, they are after solidarity, not intergenerational conflict.

This also applies to the Fridays for Future movement. It argues from the perspective of the younger generation, but then calls on the rest of society to cooperate with its vision for the future. Instead of seeking confrontation, these young activists have managed to convince their own parents and other members of the older generation to support their cause. Today, a large majority of German residents sees the fight against climate change as a priority, among them many people from older segments of the population.

The FFF strategy – closing ranks between the generations – seems to work in many countries, as demonstrated by the 2019 European elections, during which the Greens were able to make considerable gains.

Politics for every generation

From the point of view of Germany's governing parties, the younger generation seems mostly to be the cause of problems. In 2017, the leadership of the Social Democrats was faced with a growing dilemma. Kevin Kühnert, the then-chairman of their youth organisation, Jusos, warned that if the party carried on as it had, there would be nothing left for his generation within the party. In 2019, Angela Merkel's CDU faced a similar rebuke, but in the form of a viral YouTube video, called "The destruction of the CDU." A YouTuber named Rezo dissected how Germany's largest governing party had neglected every single issue related to the future – from climate change to defence policy and pressing social issues. In the subsequent 2019 European elections, first-time voters gave both the CDU and the SPD the cold shoulder in extraordinary numbers. Although their crisis management during the coronavirus pandemic helped to halt their downward spiral, both the CDU and SPD will have to find new ways to cater to the interests of the young if they want to survive after the pandemic has subsided.

In a way, the Fridays for Future movement risks falling in a "generational" trap by making the climate crisis a youth issue. The CDU and SPD must act quickly to add environmental policies to the core of their platform and to link it credibly to their traditional priorities. At the same time, they also need to address other issues which have the potential for intergenerational conflict: education, property acquisition, debt repayment and old-age provisions. No easy task when many young people feel alienated already.

Reconciling the interests of each generation is vital to the maintenance of social cohesion at both the local and national levels. The UK's EU vote does not have to be the model – there is another way. For example, Ireland voted yes on same-sex marriage during its 2015 referendum, despite the Catholic Church's strict opposition, owing in part to a somewhat different youth movement. "Call your Grannie" encouraged young people to talk to their grandparents about why they should vote yes.

A lack of this kind of intergenerational solidarity has a dramatic impact on the quality of political decisions. Under Angela Merkel, the German government scrapped its climate protection targets in 2017, favouring the interests of other segments of society than the younger generation. Similarly, the divisions in Great Britain have been reinforced since the 2016 Brexit referendum.

The only way out of this deadlock is to address intergenerational conflicts of interest head on by engaging in open public debate. Political, economic and social decisions must be "intergenerationally neutral," thus making sure that no generation is disadvantaged. FFF activists can also follow the Irish example and persuade their grandparents and older relatives to vote for their causes.

The younger generation has often had the better ideas. Since childhood, Gen Zers have learned to become experts at dealing with insecurity and uncertainty; they are also able to consider our societal ills from a new and unencumbered perspective. Older people have reacted to their plans and demands with scepticism and mistrust for far too long, and now the challenges are too urgent to ignore. It can only pay off to listen to our young people.

Notes

1 https://www.ipsos.com/ipsos-mori/en-uk/how-britain-voted-2019-election
2 Hurrelmann et al. 2019, p. 41.
3 Hurrelmann et al. 2019, p. 42.
4 Piketty 2014.
5 Friedrichs 2015.
6 SRzG Foundation 2015.
7 Neubauer and Repenning 2019, p. 58.
8 Neubauer and Repenning 2019, p. 48.
9 Wolfert und Quenzel 2019, p. 135.

Chapter 4

Climate protest versus populism
Understanding Gen Z's political orientation

FFF needs the educated middle class

An early evening rain approaches Dortmund during the Fridays for Future summer convention. Anyone not busy preparing food seeks shelter in the tent city or the ice rink at the park. There, adult activists and scientists are discussing the movement's goals with members of Fridays for Future. About 50 young people have made themselves comfortable on the floor in front of the stage.

"What do we want? Climate justice!" is the chant heard at many Fridays for Future demonstrations across the world. At the convention in Dortmund as elsewhere, many people tend to see capitalism in its present form as the main problem standing in the way of their goals. Very few believe that it will be possible to reduce greenhouse emissions to zero without fundamentally changing our current economic system.

Their rhetorical talent is impressive, as is their profound understanding of the climate crisis. While 15 to 20 percent of the younger generation sympathise with the movement, Fridays for Future draws on the political talent of about 5 percent of each age group.[1] The movement radiates far beyond the orbit of their schools; university students have long been involved with Students for Future and parents with Parents for Future. There are also Teachers for Future, Doctors for Future, Scientists for Future and so on. Fighting the climate crisis is important to many people, but they tend to attend protests less often than the hard core. That being said, both groups – the activists and the quieter sympathisers – taken together are strong enough to lend the necessary power to the protests.

Yet FFF does not represent all segments of the younger generation. Most active members of the movement are from well-educated, middle-class families, both of whom will probably have little trouble replacing old oil heating systems or commuting to work despite a CO_2 tax.

In *On the End of the Climate Crisis*, activists Luisa Neubauer and Alexander Repenning write that the climate crisis reinforces existing inequalities.[2] They cite the gilets jaunes (Yellow Vest) movement in France as an example of social upheaval caused by an unjust climate policy. "When you talk about reduction targets, you can't ignore redistribution," they write. "This is also what we mean when we demand climate justice."

Right from the start, the debate initiated by FFF has revolved around the question of how to prevent economically disadvantaged parts of society from bearing the burden inherent to the transition to a climate-neutral economy. They will likely be hit the hardest by rising costs for heating, petrol, travel and food sparked by to a CO_2 tax. Their voices however are missing from FFF's political debates. Very few young people from disadvantaged families with fewer educational opportunities feel drawn to the movement, which makes it harder for FFF to develop a vision for a "carbon neutral" society that works for all segments of its generation.

The other side of Gen Z

Cut to Frankfurt an der Oder, a city of 60,000 inhabitants on the Polish–German border, one hour due east of Berlin. The autumn sun lights up the corridor of the Konrad Wachsmann Vocational and Secondary School. The building was erected in the Bauhaus style, explains Gabriele Kohlmeyer, a biology teacher, as she points the way to a meeting room. "The corridors are on the south side. The classrooms face north, so they're nice and cool in the summer."

One needs to look no further than Frankfurt an der Oder to find young people with absolutely no connection to Fridays for Future. The school building radiates openness and transparency, which is also part of the school's concept: Many different educational avenues are offered here, from university prerequisites to practical vocational training: Carla is preparing for her final exams before going on to study psychology at university; Vanessa is anxious to complete a basic school-leaving certificate, so that she can start vocational training. All in all, more than 1,700 students attend classes at the centre. Many of them commute to school from the villages around Frankfurt an der Oder every day.

David and Anna are on track to complete the entrance requirements necessary to study social work or early childhood education. David (loose-fitting hoodie, black-rim glasses) enjoys the relaxed atmosphere at the school, which makes it easier for him to learn – "but the respect is still there," says the 17-year-old while touching his black goatee.

"Because it's still teachers and students." Anna disagrees. The 17-year-old is wearing a white strapless tank top, despite the fact it is nearly November. Her long, dark blonde hair is tied back in a tight ponytail with a scrunchy. "I've seen so many students show zero respect toward the teachers or the other students."

Brandenburg is one of four federal states in which young people can vote at age 16. In September 2019, most of the students at Konrad Wachsmann School were allowed to vote in the Brandenburg state elections that decided who would govern them for the next five years.

Anna voted. "I had imagined it differently," she says afterwards. "More modern." She stood behind a cardboard divider to mark her "x"; she had expected a real voting booth. But two months later, she is not quite sure in which election she actually voted. "I just don't understand politics," says Anna. "I pick up what I learn at school or what my father tells me." He's the only one interested in politics at home, Anna explains. "I don't think my mother understands politics."

That being said, Anna does care about certain political issues. Like so many others, environmental protection is close to her heart. The other day she saw something on television about animal testing, she says. "This is something that needs to change. A monkey belongs in nature and shouldn't be subjected to experiments in a lab." In her own life, she does what she can – like buying natural cosmetics that have not been tested on animals. So far, so typical of the young generation.

But then the conversation takes a turn. Anna mentions that she is also interested in the future of Germany. "I think we all know what I'm talking about." This time it is not climate policy. Anna wants to talk about foreigners. "I think it's slowly getting out of hand," she says, describing how she has been approached so often on the street that she hardly dares to go outside during the day. Her classmate interrupts her: He lives near a refugee centre and has never experienced any like that. Nonetheless, David does agree with Anna that climate policy and the debate surrounding migrants were by far the most important issues – before the corona pandemic and its attendant restrictions hit. Anna is clear: "I want a political party that does something for the environment and something against foreigners." In her political preferences, she is as divided as Generation Z as a whole.

Gabriele Kohlmeyer, the biology teacher, confirms that climate policy is certainly an issue for her students, reflected in the popularity of the Greens. As a teacher, she has also noticed that none of the students go to the Fridays for Future demonstrations, and that many of them sympathise with the Alternative for Germany (AfD), the right-wing populist

party. Her impressions are underscored by the recent Brandenburg parliamentary elections: The Greens were the strongest party among the 16
to 24-year-olds, with 27 percent, but the AfD followed closely behind
in second place with 18 percent of the youth vote.

For the climate and against foreigners?

Young people today are growing up in a different political climate. After
many years of complacency, young people are once again voicing their
concerns and engaging in hotly contested political debates, even within
their own ranks. Some among them welcome the entry of the AfD into
state parliaments and the Bundestag, despite – or even because of – the
right-wing populist party's opposition to immigration, minorities and
the open acceptance of refugees. Others in the same young generation
want to see the climate crisis at the top of the agenda, supporting the
Green Party and campaigning with Fridays for Future for more tolerance, a stronger European Union and sustainable agriculture.

German society is once again openly debating the direction the
country should go in and the role it should play in the world – and the
younger generation has joined in. Angela Merkel's ostensibly rational
pragmatism, which framed her political decisions as the only feasible
choice, has given way to new conflicts and ways of thinking.

Significantly more politically engaged than their predecessors, Gen Z has
contributed greatly to this development, in particular through the impact of
Fridays for Future. Generation Y, the now 20-somethings that came before
them, generally avoided major political conflicts, looking instead for pragmatic, individual solutions to political and social problems. In contrast,
young people under 20 are often in an open dialogue with their parents
about policy solutions, especially in terms of migration and the climate
crisis, and they approach issues with an open mind. Not all of these discussions are controversial; on the contrary, Anna openly admits that she
followed her father's recommendation when she voted for the first time.
However, she gave her second vote to a representative from a different
party that she had chosen herself.

She is not alone on this front. Parents have a major influence on
first-time voters, as do their friends. Sympathies for right-wing populist
or even right-wing extremist parties are by no means an isolated phenomenon or unique to the federal state of Brandenburg. In a comprehensive school in Hesse, a grade 9 class held their own European
elections. The students campaigned for different parties before voting.
The AfD received several votes; after the in-class election, most of the
class left for the Fridays for Future demonstration.

As with the rest of society, Generation Z's political spectrum has become broader. A look at Great Britain reveals even more clearly how diametrically opposed the political interests of the younger generation can be. Anyone who travels two hours north by train from London can tell a very different Brexit story from Jack, who campaigned for the remain vote in the vastly more pro-European southeast of the country.

Walking down Mexborough's High Street from the marketplace, the first thing one notices are the abandoned shop fronts. The small town in the former coal mining centre of South Yorkshire never recovered from the forced deindustrialisation under Prime Minister Margaret Thatcher. Today, the coal pit has been replaced by non-descript commercial buildings housing call centres and warehouses. These two sectors, which often barely pay a living wage, are the town's so-called future industries.

Sixty-nine percent of the local population voted to leave the European Union – one of the highest margins in the UK. Mexborough is Brexit country, even among the young. "I worked in a call centre once," says Elliot, in his mid-20s, over an evening of beer and billiards with his friends at the pub. Hard work, totally exhausting. But there are not many other jobs. "Our generation could never expect much prosperity," says his friend Jonathan. "Things can't get any worse now that we're out of the EU."

Three of the four standing around the pool table voted for Brexit. The fourth thought that it would have been better for Britain to remain in the EU, but he stayed at home that day instead of going to vote. They are in the minority within their generation, but they likely also could have tipped the scales in favour of a narrow "remain."

Five kinds of political orientation

Generation Z – a generation of cosmopolitan climate savers or the bleeding edge of a new populist wave? The concept of "a generation" can easily mask the enormous contradictions within a given generation. Anyone writing about how "today's young people tick" must be careful not to focus on individual groups. The fight against the climate crisis is clearly the topic used by particularly engaged young people to set the tone of political debate. But there are also other facets of this generation.

The refugee "crisis," the future of the European Union, the role of Islam in German society, the power of an allegedly detached and indifferent elite – in public debate, right-wing populist parties such as the Alternative for Germany, but also previously the United Kingdom Independence Party (UKIP) in Britain, have repeatedly taken on these same issues to varying effect. To determine how susceptible young people are to these messages, youth researchers presented a list of typical AfD statements to 15 to 25-year-olds, with clear results: Some groups within Gen Z are anything but immune to their appeal.[3] They think that Germany has taken in too many refugees and complain that it is impossible to make negative comments about foreigners without being called a racist. They believe that the government withholds "the truth" from the population, and many of them say that the state cares more about refugees than about Germans who need help.

Not everyone who supports some or all of these statements holds clear populist convictions. 19-year-old Markus, who is about to complete his Abitur (the German pre-university degree) in Frankfurt an der Oder, thinks it is appropriate for Germany to take in so many refugees and migrants, but also that a distinction must be made between those who flee for economic reasons and those who fear for their lives. The former should be supported in their countries of origin. When asked about freedom of speech, he says that everyone in Germany can freely express their views. "But I do think that sometimes you should be careful what you say and to whom." Markus's desire for a more nuanced debate speaks to a lively belief in democracy – more so than an affinity towards populism. In terms of other hot topics, he positions himself very clearly: Islam enriches German society, and "Without the EU, Germany would be incapable of doing much economically."

Based on studies of young people regularly conducted in Germany, five political orientations are visible within Generation Z:[4]

- *The cosmopolitans.* They reject all populist statements, authoritarian conceptions of the state and violence as a means of conflict resolution. They speak out clearly in favour of immigration to Germany. Twelve percent of 15 to 25-year-olds belong to this group.
- *The open-minded.* They are opposed to most populist and authoritarian positions and support immigration. However, every other person in this group believes it is socially inacceptable to say anything negative about foreigners without being accused of racism. One third think that the government is hiding "the truth." Twenty-seven percent belong to this group.
- *The undecided.* Twenty-eight percent of respondents want to limit immigration. They agree with economic populist statements, but reject national populist messages as well as extremism and violence.
- *The populist-curious.* They agree with most populist statements. One in two believes that a strong hand is needed to maintain law and order. Some also advocate for the use of violence in social conflicts. Twenty-four percent belong to this group.

- *The national populists.* Nine percent of respondents endorse all the standard populist statements, are in favour of a strong hand that "brings order back to our country" and are in favour of a significant drop in immigration.

All told, 39 percent of this cohort of young people fall into the category of cosmopolitans and the open-minded, while a third are inclined to populism and national populism. Twenty-eight percent are undecided and are wary of taking a clear position.

Although these political positions are spread across the young generation, irrespective of educational attainment, there are nonetheless clear tendencies: Among those who intend to go to university, 51 percent are cosmopolitan or open-minded and only 22 percent are inclined to populism or national populism, while the opposite is true for students who intend to get a secondary school-leaving certificate – 17 percent to 58 percent.

The higher the social status and the higher the intended secondary school-leaving qualifications, the more likely a young person will be cosmopolitan and tolerant. Those who come from relatively poor family backgrounds with a lower educational level are more likely to sympathise with nationalist and authoritarian positions and to be opposed to the immigration of people from other countries.

An interest in politics more widely also largely depends on educational attainment. Politics is most important to secondary school students preparing for university. Twice as many of them are interested in politics compared to the rest of their generation; those with only a basic school-leaving certificate are the least enthusiastic about politics.[5]

Success at school imparts self-confidence. Once they reach the higher grades, these students have not only learned to argue based on facts, but also to apply these skills to their activism. They can literally afford to put their energy into an altruistic fight against climate change – a phenomenon that will affect the poor much more. With their university-prep school-leaving certificates, they do not need to be worried about their futures. Their digital skills will help them find a job even in times of pandemic, which allows them to devote their time and energy to the issue of climate crisis. They have the social capital required to make their voices heard.

The situation is quite different for young people who obtain only a basic school-leaving certificate or no certificate at all. While environmental issues are important to them as well, they are also concerned with other more pressing issues than climate change: education, finding a job and making enough money. Even before the coronavirus crisis, and despite a long period of economic prosperity from the mid-2000s to

2020, they worried about not finding suitable vocational training or a job. With the continuation of the coronavirus crisis, those fears have been magnified.

Fear of downward mobility

The trend is clear: A solid education and high social status equal more open-mindedness. There are striking exceptions however: A minority, some 15 percent, of Gen Zers who come from wealthier families and are aiming for a university acceptance (or have one already) support populist ideas or think in national populist terms.[6] This phenomenon has long been observed in the older population. Writing about the AfD's counterpart in France, sociologist Didier Eribon was "convinced" in 2009 that "the election of the Front National must be interpreted, at least in part, as a last resort for people with a working-class background to defend their identity."[7] While that likely continues to be true today, the Front National in France and the AfD in Germany are no longer elected purely by workers and globalisation's supposed losers. Their ideas have also found purchase among people in the middle and upper classes afraid for their futures.

Obviously, populist attitudes develop among those who fear becoming the losers of tomorrow. This diffuse fear of downward mobility in a volatile society characterised by rapid economic and technological change points to why poor young people from disadvantaged backgrounds but also some comparatively well-off young people from the lower middle class can hold right-wing populist views. While the majority of Gen Z is very optimistic about the future, of those with a low socio-economic status, a large minority of some 30 percent fear that they will never be able to improve their social standing through their own efforts.[8] This fatalistic attitude toward one's own social mobility is also likely to open the door to populist thinking. In times of economic collapse, especially in the wake of the coronavirus pandemic, these attitudes are likely to harden even further, increasing the risk that large segments of Generation Z will become "Generation Covid."

Diversity in the young generation

All that being said, hardcore national-populists are in the minority among young people today. When Julie and Madeleine think about what characterises their generation, surprisingly, one word comes to mind: tolerance. "I'd say there is really almost no more racism in our generation," says Julie. "Not at our school, really," her classmate

Madeleine agrees. If she is approached because of the colour of her skin, then almost never by people of her own generation. It used to be much more unusual in Germany to see people from other, non-white, backgrounds, says Julie. "My father is Black. He used to really attract attention walking down the street."

Julie's view may well be influenced by her personal environment. The 15-year-old attends the bilingual section of Sophie Scholl Secondary School in Berlin, one of the most popular schools in the tolerant capital. "I'm happy to live in Berlin," she says. But even beyond Berlin, it has become natural for the younger generation to have friends or classmates whose parents were born in other countries. Today, 30 percent of young people have a history of migration in their immediate family background – and half of them have a German passport. This has an impact. According to the German youth study, 79 percent would not object to a refugee family moving in next door to them. Nonetheless, 11 percent would still have problems with a family from Africa, 9 percent with homosexual neighbours and 8 percent with a Jewish family next door.[9]

Celina from Giessen also knows more than enough about discrimination, especially from her parents. Her father came to Germany from Cameroon 35 years ago to study. Her mother is the daughter of Turkish guest workers. "They've experienced a lot of it," the 14-year-old says. "Back then everything was different in Germany." Today, no one would approach her to insult her openly. But she still notices "small things" now and then. That is one of the reasons why Celina wants to make it big in her chosen career one day: "If I'm independent and no one can control me, then I don't care if someone is racist," she says, "because then no one can bring me down, no matter what they think."

Between Generation Greta and Generation Covid

Ultimately, the main factors that divide Gen Z stem from different political attitudes, along with differing educational and employment opportunities. On one end of the spectrum, there are the politically active, committed (and mostly female) cosmopolitans heavily invested in an environmental perspective, a group that could be called "Generation Greta." On the other end, there are those (mostly young men) left behind with poor or no educational qualifications, from low economic status or even precarious homes with real feelings of insecurity and dissatisfaction. The lower their social standing and education level, the more sceptical they are of society's inherent fairness and justice. Increasing economic inequality brough about by the coronavirus pandemic could turn this group into a lost "Generation Covid."

Between these two extremes is "Generation Undecided." They have a fairly good education, are optimistic about their professional futures and enjoy the privileges that being part of a middle-class family provides. Many of them aspire to a lifestyle similar to that of their parents, preferably with the same house, garden and white picket fence. Their level of political interest is moderate; their participation marginal.

The most committed and those left behind have coalesced to symbolise the breadth of this generation's public image. The committed – especially through their participation in Fridays for Future – have created a powerful future-oriented political movement; in contrast, those left behind have gained political purchase by being, in a prosperous and affluent society, unafraid to voice their profound dissatisfaction with prevailing conditions and to violate the unwritten rules of political correctness.

Back at their convention in Dortmund, the Fridays for Future activists chant, "We are young, we are here, we want a future without fear!" Meanwhile, on Dortmund's southern ring road, everything has come to a standstill. About 20 young people have blocked the inner-city ring road. As traffic backs up, drivers have enough time to read the placards lining the road: "We spoke, act now!" Then, one of the organisers suddenly shouts, "It's time!" and the group obediently stands up and clears the road.

Fridays for Future was born middle-class. The protest is cheerful. Men wear glitter on their cheeks and accuse politicians of gambling away their futures by doing nothing in the fight against climate change.

Cities like Dortmund are difficult ground for the movement. The Ruhr region, with Dortmund at its centre, has not yet recovered from its own deindustrialisation and the turn away from coal mining and car production, and now FFF is already pushing for the next major economic restructuring. Although the phase-out of the coal industry has long been under way, the unemployment rate is still higher here than elsewhere in the country and more people live in relative poverty than in the rest of Germany. In some parts of Dortmund's north side, social cohesion is on the verge of collapse.

Students aiming for university, mostly young women, constitute the majority of the participants at the climate demonstration in Dortmund. Even students from the private Waldorf school are in attendance. But there is no sign of students from the regular secondary schools – only Generation Greta has met up here.

Notes

1 Wahlström et al. 2019.
2 Neubauer and Repenning 2019, p. 184.
3 Schneekloth and Albert 2019, p. 77.

4 Schneekloth and Albert 2019, p. 79.
5 Schneekloth and Albert 2019, p. 51.
6 Schneekloth and Albert 2019, p. 81.
7 Eribon 2009, p. 134.
8 Köcher et al. 2019, p. 26.
9 Schneekloth and Albert 2019, p. 89.

Chapter 5

No interest in party politics
Why do Gen Z feel alienated?

Friday morning is market day for Eberswalde, a town of some 40,000 inhabitants, a 30-minute train ride from Berlin. Around noon, the smell of charcoal grills and Thuringian bratwurst permeates the air. Some stands sell fresh fruit and vegetables, while others make a bid to discount the last of their summer fashion. Between the stands, an umbrella with the logo of the Social Democratic Party (SPD) shines bright red in the August sun.

It's late August 2019, and Brandenburg is two days away from state elections. The sparsely populated and not particularly wealthy state is shaped like a huge donut, with the capital city Berlin carved out of the centre. That upcoming Sunday, Member of the State Parliament Hardy Lux intends to defend his seat in the Brandenburg state legislature against the right-wing populist party AfD. He will eventually win with barely a 0.6 percent lead on his opponent. This Friday morning, he is campaigning hard for any last undecided voters.

Among many other people, Lux will owe his extremely narrow victory to Kurt. Last night, the 19-year-old member of the SPD's youth organisation went door to door, sticking flyers into mailboxes and ringing doorbells. Today, he is handing out red roses in the market with a charming smile.

In particular, Kurt has to address the concerns of the older generations if the Social Democrats want to remain the strongest party in Brandenburg. His own generation's vote carries little weight in these elections. In the last national election in 2017, only 15 percent of voters were between the ages of 18 and 30; more than twice as many were over 60. As German society continues to age, the proportion of older people will continue to grow, creating an even larger discrepancy by the time of the next national elections in 2021. The federal state of Brandenburg, where Kurt has been campaigning, has seen an exodus of young people in recent decades: Most shoppers here at the market are pensioners, which makes it an ideal spot for doing some political outreach.

People like Kurt are rare for yet another reason. In Europe today, significantly less than one percent of Gen Z belongs to a political party; Germany is no exception. Although a third of this generation is interested in becoming politically active, their involvement takes place outside of party politics. According to youth studies, 12 to 25-year-olds rank political parties last when asked what social institutions they trust most. That said, banks, churches and large companies also score very poorly.[1]

The younger generation believes in democracy. Yet, they obviously do not feel that their concerns are in good hands when left to party politicians. In their view, political parties represent a rigid, bureaucratic apparatus of power that revolves only around itself. They also think of them as seniors' clubs, and rightfully so: The membership of the CDU/CSU and SPD is, on average, 60 years old; the Greens clock in at 50, and the AfD somewhere in-between. The same applies to members of the liberal FDP and the left-wing Die Linke.

Kurt remains undaunted. When he joined the "Jusos," the SPD's youth wing, at the age of 16, he was the only one at his school to join the Social Democrats – or any party's youth organisation for that matter. In this respect, young people are even more reluctant than the older generations, for whom party membership is not exactly trendy either. CDU/CSU, SPD, FDP and Die Linke have all lost more than half of their members since 1990. Only the Greens, established in 1983, and the AfD, founded in 2013, have enjoyed an increase in their membership rolls. A total of 1.2 million people in Germany are currently members of a party, just under 1.5 percent of the population. In 1990, the figure stood at three percent.

Not only political parties lack substantial input from younger people: Organisations and institutions that require official registration are equally unattractive. Youth organisations within trade unions, churches, welfare organisations and sports clubs are not doing any better. Clearly, the young generation wants to be independent and is looking for more flexible forms of participation.

While Kurt is campaigning for the SPD in Eberswalde's market square, the local Fridays for Future demonstration passes by. "People from my school, who I always thought had nothing to do with party politics, are now joining Fridays for Future and are really getting involved," he says. "This proves to me that our generation was never as apolitical as people thought."

Kurt's generation is certainly not apolitical, it is just not interested in political parties. With their involvement in Fridays for Future, the young generation has not only demonstrated that engagement in a social movement feels more effective to them than party participation, but also that political parties have a lot of work to do in trying to win them back.

The Merkel generation

Gen Zers are coming into their own at the end of a political era in Germany. As early as 2015, the news magazine *Der Spiegel* pointed out that young first-time voters had never participated in a federal election in which Angela Merkel was not elected chancellor. She had always just been there. If Greta Thunberg had been born in Germany, only the first two of her 17 years would have been under a chancellor other than Merkel.

And yet, neither Generation Y nor Generation Z elected Angela Merkel as chancellor. Her party is not particularly popular among the younger generations. In the 2019 European elections, the governing CDU and SPD received only a combined 20 percent of the votes among 18 to 24-year-olds. Among the over 60-year-olds, the figure was almost three times as high.

The traditional ruling parties in Germany, the CDU and the SPD, who have dominated political life in the country since the post-war period, are losing ground. This vote of no confidence is even felt within party politics. "There's no plan for the future," according to Kurt, the young Social Democrat. In his view, politicians are too timid about using new technologies – which goes back to the issue of their age. "You just don't think the same way at 60 as you do at 20."

Although Kurt thinks that Fridays for Future's positions are too radical, he believes that FFF is right to tell politicians, "Hey, you can't continue moving as slowly as you are now." Climate policy is an existential issue that simply cannot be put off. "Politicians procrastinate too much."

"Young voters are not important to the major political parties," agrees an FFF activist in Ludwigsburg near Stuttgart. Generation Z's distrust of politics extends far beyond Fridays for Future supporters. "I just find it strange that so many old people make so many decisions on behalf of younger people," says 15-year-old Emil.

When asked whether politicians take sufficient account of the issues affecting the younger generation, Paul's answer is clear: "No, not at all." Apart from their failure to tackle the climate crisis, he believes that there are no plans for digitalisation and education policies. CDU and SPD compensate their poor results among young voters with the votes of the old, says Paul. "It's a problem when for the last 20 years, policy has been made for 60-year-olds. You really notice it."

Kurt shares Paul's analysis. "Young people are demographically irrelevant," he says, despite being a member of the Social Democratic youth organisation himself. He recently read that the average age of voters in the last three state elections in East Germany was 55. "It totally scared me. Of course, we're being ignored!"

"It's no wonder that the turnout among young people is much lower than that of their grandparents if they only have the choice between the old white man in suit A and the old white man in suit B," write the young members of the Youth Council Generations Foundation in their book *You Don't Have a Plan, That's Why We're Making One*. The age discrepancy is so huge that it is difficult to feel represented. "None of these politicians seem to understand the concerns of young people."[2]

In Germany, 71 percent of 15 to 25-year-olds agree with the statement "I don't think politicians care what people like me think." Eighty-four percent think that young people should have more of a say in politics.[3] In short, almost an entire generation thinks it is not being heard.

David did not go to the polls. He generally supports the right of 16-year-olds to vote in the state of Brandenburg. "I knew I had a voice, I am important, I can achieve something," says the 17-year-old, but then adds: "I know politics is important, but somehow I just wasn't interested."

An election in Brandenburg, however, has hardly ever been as exciting as it was in 2019, when the election campaign threatened to polarise this federal state. Social Democrats have been in power in this mostly rural state since reunification, but some polls indicated that the right-wing populist AfD stood a chance of becoming the largest party in the state parliament – a development that was, until recently, unthinkable. David stayed home anyway. For him, politicians have a communication problem: "All they ever do is talk to each other and then decide something. They need to come up with a new perspective."

For Luzia, not voting was never an option. Politics is deeply important to the 16-year-old: She has been co-organising climate protests in Aschaffenburg from the beginning. Over time, however, she has also become increasingly frustrated by the inactivity of the federal government and the parties within it. "I truly believed that if we took to the streets by the thousands and protested over and over, the message might get through," Luzia says. "I had hoped that politicians would change their policies. After all, they always say that the people have the power." After thinking it over for a moment, she adds, "maybe that was a bit naive."

This assessment is tantamount to a rebuke of Merkel's term in office. Even the chancellor finds it difficult to sell her climate policy as a success. Fridays for Future has "certainly pushed the federal government to accelerate matters," she admitted in summer 2019, when her cabinet passed a climate package after years of hesitation. In fact, the movement "was a further reason for us to take a more determined approach to the matter." What Merkel did not mention was that she had taken office in 2005 as the self-declared "climate chancellor" and had resolved to make environmental policy an absolute priority of her time in office.

From the perspective of the climate activists in the younger generation, only one thing has prevailed when it comes to environmental issues: a complete and total standstill. Companies such as the car giant Volkswagen, the energy supplier RWE, technology behemoth Siemens or Deutsche Bank have an outsized influence on German politics, Luzia believes. "I underestimated the power of the lobbyists. In the end, economic and political interests are intertwined." She admits that it is a success that climate policy is now being discussed as much as it is, "but I'm afraid that talking is all it is. It won't bring down CO_2 emissions."

For some segments of Generation Z, the influence exerted by lobbyists on political life is a major obstacle. An FFF activist in Ludwigsburg, for example, criticised Transport Minister Andreas Scheuer: "I think he's more concerned with economic interests than with climate protection." When the minister attended a public discussion on the "mobility of the future" with 450 guests at an event hall, six FFF activists between the ages of 16 and 18 marched up to the front and chanted the Fridays for Future slogan "We are young, we are here, we want a future without fear!" A video shows an elderly attendee trying to hold his hand over the mouth of one activist to silence them. In the end, the police carried the group out of the hall.

Dwindling trust in governing parties

In times of crisis, the vast majority of Germans, even the younger ones, traditionally stand behind their government. The two governing parties benefited from this in 2020, during the coronavirus pandemic, but this support is unlikely to last. Confidence in the governing coalition's ability to solve urgent social problems has been on the wane for years among all segments of Gen Z. The engaged members of the FFF movement remain frustrated because the measures they consider vitally necessary are not being implemented quickly or consistently enough; the socially disadvantaged are angry because they feel ignored and disconnected from the political process; the undecided feel insecure about the future.

This is not just a German phenomenon. The parliamentary system that coalesced in the post-war period is undergoing significant changes in many West European countries, including Great Britain, the Netherlands, Italy, France and Spain. And it is not just young people who feel that the old systems are no longer working in the face of globalisation and digitalisation. The decline of traditional political parties and the success of populist voices are closely related to this development and are symptoms of a larger democratic crisis.

Andreas Reckwitz, a German sociologist, sees a paradigm shift in Europe's democratic societies. Since the 1980s, economic deregulation has been accompanied by a rise in individual rights: This has meant on the one hand that market globalisation, the erosion of workers' rights and the privatisation of state services, and, on the other, more rights for women, migrants, gay, lesbian and trans people and a new diversity in socially accepted ways of life. But this liberal paradigm has now been plunged into a profound crisis. "The rise of populism is a symptom of this crisis."[4] Not only is the neoliberal economic model under severe pressure, but so are the rights of women, migrants and homosexuals, among others. So recently won, they are suddenly up for debate again, fueled by the divisive rhetoric of various populist parties.

In these complicated times, the younger generation is certainly willing and able to engage in fresh thinking and provide new ideas to solve existing social problems, without first having to work through existing convictions and prejudices. Gen Zers are much more eager than the older generations to give ostensibly unconventional approaches their serious consideration.

And Gen Zers are not single-issue voters and thinkers, interested only in solving the climate crisis. Twenty-five-year-old Jakob Novotný, for example, is running for mayor under the slogan "Rent – Climate – Education" in Ludwigsburg, an eighteenth-century baroque residential town north of Stuttgart with some 100,000 inhabitants. From Jakob's point of view, the two candidates ahead of him in the polls have not even addressed the most important issues facing constituents. Which is why he has also thrown his hat in the ring.

Walking through town, Novotný notes which streets belong to which investor. "What is being built here by private developers are exclusively ultra-expensive, luxury apartments and properties," he says, pointing to a modern townhouse on the edge of the historic city centre. In contrast, between 1990 and 2017, Ludwigsburg neglected to construct any social housing of its own. "There's definitely something wrong here."

"Actually, it's quite obvious what we have to do in terms of the housing shortage, to stop the bubble that is slowly expanding here," he says. Investment in real estate should simply cease being profitable. "The government, the city, the legislature should ensure that the urban population has somewhere to live, and not that investors can make serious cash from housing."

Novotný's decision to run for mayor as an independent candidate was spontaneous. He shot a video, set up a website, started a Facebook campaign and canvassed the streets of the city centre, presenting his views on the housing crisis, the climate crisis and the crisis in education. In the end, he managed to garner nearly 9 percent of the votes, a more than respectable result for a political newcomer.

A choice between two axes

Generation Z favours political parties and candidates that authentically advocate for clear policies. Their preferences are clearly reflected in their general disinterest in the big mainstream parties (the conservative CDU and the progressive Social Democrats). The environmentally oriented Greens have benefited from this situation, as young voters reward them for their stance on the climate crisis. The Greens have also managed to craft a modern and open-minded image through their relatively small party apparatus, which makes them seem less staid and bureaucratic than other parties. In contrast, the right-wing populist AfD has taken second place among young voters, also far ahead of the CDU and SPD. A closer look nonetheless reveals that the younger generation's diverging interests in the Greens and the AfD are not cut from the same cloth: While the youngest voter segment propelled the Greens to their best result ever, the AfD is most popular in the 30 to 50-year-old age group. The choice between cosmopolitanism and national populism has replaced the traditional left-right pattern of conservatism versus progressiveness that has long prevailed among young people of preceding generations.

Despite their status as the two long-standing governing parties, the CDU and SPD are having difficulty attracting the attention of young people, the majority of whom consider them bland and impersonal. What they lack are clear statements and fresh perspectives. To most young people, both parties only seem interested in holding on to power, instead of tackling pressing challenges. Looking at their style and demeanour, both parties do not exactly come across as modern and up to date.

Young people want political parties to communicate clear platforms, positions and priorities, although many are also concerned about how that kind of rigidity could lead to a polarisation of society. In youth studies in Germany, 56 percent of young people say that the growing hostility between people with different opinions scares them.[5]

"Sometimes we get to the point in our circle of friends where we have to be careful that we don't end up in a fight," says Markus from Frankfurt an der Oder. Nevertheless, he still maintains a relationship with a friend who voted for the AfD. "I told her that I don't think it's a good idea and I don't support it," the 19-year-old says. "But I think that's one of the things that defines friendship, being able to have different views and still talk to each other."

Carla's circle of friends in Frankfurt an der Oder covers the entire political spectrum. They all voted for different parties, says the 16-year-old secondary school student. After the election, "some people got into it because they didn't think the other person's opinion was okay." But to her, it is important to listen to others. "I don't like it when people stop being friends just because they have different opinions." For Carla, that also applies to politics; the other parties shouldn't shun the AfD "just because they don't like the idea of them."

In the end, it seems that for some Gen Zers, politics is actually less divisive than it is for much of the rest of society. With her dyed black hair and oversized yellow knit sweater, no one would doubt Lara when she says that she belongs to the political left in Frankfurt, but her circle of friends also includes people with right-wing views. "I like them as a person, but we don't discuss politics. After all, you talk about different things with different friends, anyway."

Politics for Generation Z

Like each generation before it, Generation Z is not a uniform demographic group. That said, parties that do not include environmental issues and the climate crisis in their platforms will have trouble gaining support from young people. The Green Party is thus ideally positioned to attract young voters, and membership in their youth organisation is consequently on the rise. For the Generation Greta subgroup, climate policy has become the litmus test for how much a party takes the protection of the natural environment seriously or – as Luzia puts it – the extent to which that party gives in to the interests of the car industry, agri-businesses and the energy companies.

By contrast, economic issues also remain important for young people, especially with regard to their own careers and earning potential. In most European countries, Gen Zers were pretty relaxed about their personal futures until the outbreak of the coronavirus pandemic. With the continued deterioration of the economy due to Covid-19, the issue will become more prominent in their political worldview. It is up to all political parties to provide credible answers, instead of ceding the terrain to the populists.

On the list of Gen Z's most pressing issues, the environment and employment opportunities are followed by education, digitalisation, work-life balance, housing costs, property acquisition and old-age provisions. In an ideal world, existing political parties would sit down together with the young generation to develop policies that address these issues.

Young people go into an election asking themselves how choosing a particular party or a particular candidate will directly benefit them. They want to see that their vote makes a difference. This rational and goal-oriented attitude will continue to gain ground in the coming years, as long-term party bonds weaken further, and no party will be able to win voters based only on loyalty and sympathy. Going forward, political parties must convince voters each and every time that they have addressed the right issue in the right manner.

Any 17-year-old who joins a German party today will automatically end up in a seniors' club, in which baby boomers, now aged between 50 and 65, dominate. It is almost impossible to find a Gen Zer interested in becoming the secretary of a local party branch. Most of them feel alienated by the rigid structures and procedures of party events and miss the use of digital channels and fast and flexible voting.

Young people are an impatient audience, easily frustrated by the complexities of political decision-making. If political parties want Generation Z to take an active part, they must first get through to them. In other words, they need to establish modern channels of communication, public forums and discussion events to allow a look behind the curtain at the daily work of party politics. By helping to reduce Generation Z's contact anxiety with party politics, they might be able to attract a few more young people to join their ranks.

Another option would be for parties, like other social institutions, to offer internships for young people to experience political work from the inside. Party youth organisations can play an important role in this integration.

But the overarching goal of party work should be to attract young members. To this end, trial memberships, possibly even for a limited period, could be offered. Those young people who eventually decide to become long-term members should then be promoted to more responsible positions as soon as possible. This could be done through a binding youth quota based on the gender quota model: In such a model, political parties make a voluntary commitment to reserve 20 percent of the party tickets in an election for young people under the age of 30. Currently, only about 8 percent of the candidates up for election in Germany are under the age of 30. Such a youth quota would give this generation considerably more weight and allow for party reform from the inside out. Only parties that remain attractive to young members would then continue to attract good candidates.

At the same time, the minimum voting age must be lowered. The time is right for electoral reform, considering the many students under 18 who actively participate – with a great deal of skill and commitment – in the FFF movement and who have shown a remarkable ability to learn about and digest complicated issues. In short, young women and men today are able to assess, from the age of 12, what issues and alternatives are at stake in the election of a party or candidate.

Therefore, a reduction of the general minimum voting age to 16 or 14 could well be justified. It would force parties to address the concerns of this younger age group in their electoral campaigns and encourage young people to actively involve themselves in exploring the various political alternatives on offer. In 2007, Austria became the first European country to take this step by reducing the voting age to 16 in all elections.

Young people and their fresh ideas are a healthy component of a functioning democracy, but Generation Z is not always taken seriously. Christian Lindner, chairman of Germany's liberal FDP, advised Fridays for Future to leave the fight against the climate crisis to "the professionals." Similarly, during his election campaign in Ludwigsburg, Jakob Novotný was often talked down to and told that he was too young for the office of mayor. The 25-year-old is well aware of the huge discrepancies between the generations. For one, labour conditions were considerably better in the 1970s and 1980s. "Then globalisation and privatisation came along. They hit the young generation hard and, as a result, older people are on average better off," says Novotný. "They're also used to the system and go to the polls in much greater numbers than younger people."

Notes

1 Schneekloth and Albert et al. 2019, p. 93.
2 Jugendrat 2020, p. 150.
3 Schneekloth and Albert 2019, p. 94.
4 Reckwitz 2018.
5 Schneekloth and Albert 2019, p. 56.

Chapter 6

The digital virtuosos
The power of media for communication and organisation

Multimedia youth

"No, not that one, not that one either..." Lotta is carefully scrolling through the zillions of videos on her phone. The 11-year-old is sitting on a couch in the chill room of a girls' youth club, her smartphone dangling from a cord around her neck. "Here it is!" She taps the screen again, and suddenly RnB starts to blare from the speaker. On the shiny display, Lotta and her friend Finja (nine) are dancing to the rhythm – in, over and around a cardboard box. The video speeds up; the movements of the two girls seem frantic and choppy, before it abruptly slows down as the bodies of the young dancers glide almost weightlessly through the youth club in slow motion.

Fifteen seconds, then it is over. Fifteen seconds is the limit for videos on TikTok, the wildly popular social network from China. The girls recorded the clip a few hours ago. "I did the camera work!" exclaims their friend Emma with pride. Some skateboards donated to the youth club earlier that afternoon lay neatly arranged in a corner, ignored. Instead, the cardboard boxes they had arrived in served as the set for the girls' video shoot. In the cold autumn weather, the girls prefer to be creative digitally rather than skating outside.

Gen Zers are often described as digital natives, born into a digital world instead of having to learn how to navigate it. Apple introduced the iPhone in 2007; the first Android phones were launched a year later. Thus, even the oldest Generation Zers might have played around on the first iPhone at the tender age of seven, the younger ones even earlier. They can swipe back and forth between various apps in their sleep. For many of them, reaching for their smartphone is the first and the last thing they do every day – if their parents allow it.

On the face of it, the professionalism exhibited by Fridays for Future activists or young protesters in interviews and news reports might be surprising, but that dance video at the youth club is likely part of the explanation as to where they got it from. In the 1960s, shortly before his breakthrough, Andy Warhol hired a photographer to accompany him wherever he went for a year. He regularly reviewed the pictures and slowly developed a feeling for the effect he had in front of the camera. When, later, the media began to fling itself at him, Warhol was ready: He knew exactly how to shape his image through his posture and facial expression. What took Warhol a year of concerted effort (and the money to pay for a photographer!) is now accessible to everyone on their smartphones.

According to the internet journalist Sascha Lobo, the thoroughly digitalised existence of this younger generation has basically primed them through a near constant process of media training. Unlike Warhol, they are their own photographers. "An average 16-year-old has already spent hundreds of hours speaking into a camera, always matching their communication with its public response," writes Lobo.[1] "And if you've published hundreds of Instagram stories and seen the reactions, you've got a feeling for what works in the media and what doesn't."

Compared to earlier generations, Generation Z are no longer mere pioneers in the use of digital technology. They have become the virtuosos. Mobile communication and social media have lost their ultimate fascination, as the digital world has become self-evident and ubiquitous. In the weeks and months when schools were closed and face-to-face contact with friends was limited due to the coronavirus pandemic, living digitally became even more natural. In Germany – and this is typical for all European countries – 95 percent of 12-year-olds have their own smartphone, and as they get older, that number rises even further. When asked what she is doing on her phone, 13-year-old Charlotte just smiles, "What people usually do with their mobile phone." That is enough of an answer.

That being said, navigating the internet safely is anything but self-evident. The intense debate surrounding the dangers of the digital world that has raged for years now is anything but settled, and Generation Z is growing up at a time when the very structure of the internet of the future is being renegotiated. After years of open communication, the four largest – American – tech conglomerates (Facebook, Amazon, Apple and Alphabet/Google) increasingly dominate the world wide web. Sites and services owned and operated by Facebook and Google – such as WhatsApp, YouTube and Instagram – now account for the vast majority of all internet traffic, and their market share has continued to increase.

Although almost everyone can access most of the web through their mobile phone's internet browser, apps that lead only to a single specific network dominate. In some countries of the Global South – such as Indonesia – a clear majority of respondents say they use Facebook on a regular basis. Surprisingly, this majority also says that they have never been on the internet. For them, Facebook is not the internet; it is a world of its own. This unexpected response is likely also due to the fact that in many non-European markets, the lack of net neutrality means that it is cheaper to use Facebook and other social media outlets than other websites. It is therefore becoming increasingly difficult for other businesses to find users for their own products.

Among numerous other consequences, the coronavirus pandemic has demonstrated just how dependent our societies are on these global monopolies. In addition, the excitement economy inherent to social networks is changing our social debates. The war in Ukraine, the migration crisis and the election of Donald Trump in the United States have all highlighted the dangers of fake news and hate speech for our democracies. Current technology is able to create deep fakes, in which the manipulation of videos, pictures or language is often impossible to detect.

The share of US corporate profits made online is immense. According to various estimates, Facebook and Google together practically control the global market in digital advertising outside China. This monopoly is an essential threat to the internet's transparency and traditional media's ability to act as a safeguard for democratic dialogue. Due to the extraordinary destruction of their advertising revenues, quality media such as newspapers and magazines have struggled to develop new business models: Quality journalism is nearly impossible to finance under current conditions.

With the ever-increasing dominance of internet corporations, there are also growing concerns about personal data security and privacy. "On average, parents with children aged zero to 13 share 71 photos and 29 videos of their child every year to social media sites," writes Anne Longfield, the Children's Commissioner for the British government.[2] By the time they become teenagers, there will have been 1,300 posts about them online, not including those shared on private messaging apps or shared private online albums. The amount of information literally explodes once they become active on social media themselves. According to the report, children post 26 times a day on average – a total of about 70,000 posts by age 18.

Moreover, paediatricians and youth psychologists regularly issue near-apocalyptic warnings about the dangers of smartphones for younger people's physical and mental development.[3] Arthritis in the thumb joints, severe spinal defects, myopia and deafness seem harmless compared to the various psychological and depressive disorders they witness during their consultations.

Despite all these challenges, most Generation Zers have found ways to use digital technology for their own development. They are almost always one step ahead of their elders.

In 2002, 26 percent of 12 to 25-year-olds in Germany listed "surfing the internet" as a frequent activity; in 2019, the figure was 50 percent.[4] Most young people use the internet for a wide range of activities, but especially for accessing social networks and listening to music. Analyses show that communication with friends is the most important element, but information gathering is almost equally important. This is particularly true for young people from the upper social classes with good educational prospects, who go online to search for information relevant to their schooling, vocational training and working lives.

Between competence and addiction

"I've often told my daddy that I don't like his mobile phone," was the title of a collection of interviews with children about their parents' smartphone addiction conducted by the *Süddeutsche Zeitung* in its weekend supplement.[5] "Daddy really is a phone freak," complains seven-year-old Lilly. "If you wait too long to ask, 'Will you play with me?' he looks at it again. I can't always think of games that fast." Martha, also seven years old, concludes, "If I ever have a daughter, she should hide my mobile phone from me – and only tell me where it is in an emergency." Martha thinks it is stupid when parents do not listen because they are on their phones. After all, children sometimes also have important things to say, she explains.

Some Gen Zers are ahead of the game. Especially the well-educated among the post-millennials – an increasing number of whom are voluntarily restricting their own smartphone use – could easily coach their parents. "No social media. I don't have it." Julian, who is studying physics at Giessen University, only uses WhatsApp. "No Facebook, no Instagram. That ate up too much of my time." Three or four years ago, he was on Facebook on a regular basis. In the beginning, he actively engaged on the platform, posting and replying; later on, he just read along – until he started at university. "You catch yourself sitting in a lecture, scrolling through Facebook." After all, lectures aren't always that exciting. "But at the end of the day, you're just looking at nonsense," Julian recalls. "I saw no added value in it for me."

"I'd like to get rid of social media entirely," says Nicolas, a fellow student. Not only because it is a waste of time, but because of the lack of data protection. "If you look at where our information ends up, it's pretty frightening." Nicolas got rid of Instagram. "There's no limit to what you can look at. You can find a lot of things that might be funny or interesting," he adds, "but you don't really get any benefit from it."

"I'm not on Instagram or WhatsApp," Celina says. "It stressed me out all the time. It was always going ping, ping, ping!" She was not that great at answering, says the 14-year-old from Giessen. "Then I decided to quit altogether, because all it otherwise does is bother me."

Julian, Nicolas and Celina are still the exception. Ninety-four percent of their peers use messenger services like WhatsApp or Telegram every day. Four out of five young people log in to a social network or YouTube at least once a day. One in two logs in even more often. But scepticism is growing: 60 percent criticise the lack of data protection and consider hate speech and fake news to be a serious problem. They also criticise that Google and Facebook earn a lot of money with their data. Almost a third of youth survey respondents would like to be online less often in the future. One in six state that they spend so much time on the internet that there is not enough time for other things.[6]

Using a smartphone with confidence, without feeling it has a hold over you, nonetheless remains a challenge for young people. Much depends on parental influence. "When I'm online, I'm hooked for a while," says Celina self-critically. But her parents have restricted her mobile phone use to one and a half hours per day. Originally, it was supposed to be an hour. "But that wasn't enough." In other families, the kids have to surrender their phones to their parents at 6 p.m. Often that turns into 7 or 8 p.m., Celina's classmate Nele says, but overall, it works well.

Exercise in self-discipline

It is not that easy for everyone. Anna is currently doing her vocational degree at the Konrad Wachsmann School in Frankfurt an der Oder and plans to become a film editor. The 17-year-old is already shooting and editing videos with her iPad, although she has never posted her work publicly. So far, she is her only audience.

"I can't understand how people are addicted to their mobile phones nowadays," says Anna. "At school, one can manage to put away one's mobile phone during class." A few people in her class keep their smartphones on their desks at all times, she explains, even though it is forbidden.

But then, she confesses, "At home – I admit it – I'm on the phone a lot." She watches YouTube videos. However, she spends most of her time on the AFK Arena game app, an action card game. The games portal Bluestacks writes, "AFK is deceivingly simple: It lures you with the illusion of casual, carefree fun, but once you reach the most difficult stages, it ruthlessly pulls the rug out from under your feet." "I've already spent money on it," says Anna and hesitates a moment. When asked about the amount she laughs, "A lot. A hundred [euros], easily." Sometimes you need that to get ahead. Then she thinks for a second and says, "I admit: I'm addicted." Homework is often forgotten in the process. "First this is interesting, then that. Then it's evening all of a sudden, and I haven't done my homework."

Thus, smartphone use divides the generation. Success at school and in vocational training today correlates among other things with the ability of young people to decide for themselves what helps them advance and what slows them down. Young people with a sound educational background have learned to suppress the impulse to reach for their phone at critical moments. When in doubt, they log off from Instagram and Co. for a while instead of risking bad grades. Juliane Westphal, head teacher at a school in Berlin, observes that especially girls who are preparing for the exams that will allow them to attend university often do without. Some of them even get rid of their phones entirely and write letters or play cards instead. Having themselves just escaped the maelstrom of the digital world, they become worried that younger schoolmates are spending too much time online.

Playing online games, for example. At dawn, four armed fighters wade through a lake, before crossing a picturesque field. From a mountain top, their gaze wanders over the whole of the island before they quickly realise they are not alone. While fighting against other teams, gas stations explode; at the same time, the island itself becomes smaller and smaller as the game progresses.

This is how the trailer for Fortnite Chapter 2 begins, currently the most popular computer game among Generation Z. Fortnite is a so-called "co-op survival game." Its characters are colourful, the landscape pleasant – at least at the beginning.

Twelve to 19-year-olds spend 103 minutes a day playing in the virtual world; boys estimate their playing time at 146 minutes, girls at 57. Only 11 percent of them have never played an online game. Video gaming usually reaches its peak during the earlier stages of adolescence. Sports – whether organised or informal – are becoming less important by comparison, which leads to the lack of exercise often lamented among young people. Reading books is also becoming less common, irrespective of whether the text is on paper or on an e-reader. But the stereotypical image of the lonely gamer in front of his device does not apply to the majority of Gen Zers. Fifty-seven percent talk to fellow players about topics unrelated to the game in virtual TeamSpeak.[7]

Nevertheless, too many young people treat the wide range of online offers carelessly. The appeal is enormous, making it difficult for parents to limit their children's time on the web. Platforms and video games seem to spark a built-in psychological dependence, an addiction mechanism. Silicon Valley has developed algorithms with incentive programmes that provide users with a clever mix of rewards and credit points but also alarm signals, leaving them in a state of constant, intense inner excitement that keeps them hooked to their phones.[8] Users feel compelled to proceed to the next level because they think they will not be able to relax otherwise. But the opposite is true; they simply feel more restless.

That being said, the majority of young people cope well with digital challenges. They have managed to avert the risks of over-dosing on digital impulses. Contrary to the recommendations made by some psychologists and psychiatrists, this has not been achieved by banning the use of smartphones and laptops at home, but by learning and practising appropriate use of these devices, platforms and games. Their parents have helped them to set limits for themselves, to take time off and to control their screen time. Despite the tremendous psychological temptations of the virtual world, only a minority of young people neglect their real-life friends, school or non-virtual hobbies.

Just as they have learned to deal with addictive substances – the consumption of alcohol and tobacco is at an all-time low in the younger generation – Generation Z has learned to successfully deal with potential non-material, behavioural addictions, managing to escape the consumer retention algorithms.

Beyond the majority of competent youth, however, there is a much too large group of young people who find it difficult to navigate the maze of digital temptations. An estimated 30 percent of Generation Z, mostly young men, sometimes get caught up in a cycle of addiction, although it is possible to break free from it after a while. Their mental health and interpersonal skills are at risk as such a digital addiction causes them to be quickly distracted and nervous. Due to their numerous virtual contacts, they are no longer able to properly react to real-life social situations, to observe rules of courtesy or to meet their counterparts face to face. Finding it difficult to concentrate, their performance in school also decreases.

For some of them, probably two to three percent of each cohort, the addictive potential of commercial applications is too high and they begin to suffer from an internet addiction disorder or a gaming disorder as defined by the World Health Organisation.

A network for each purpose

Even in the pre-digital era, the act of cultivating friendships took on different forms. Good friends met every day in the afternoon, talked regularly on the phone or even wrote letters to each other. Others were happy to receive an occasional postcard from a friend on holiday. The Canadian band Arcade Fire – part of Generation X – describes its members' analogue youth in the song "We used to wait": Back then, they "used to wait" until letters reached their destination. And they slept at night, "before the flashing lights settled deep in my brain."

In contrast, Generation Z is not used to waiting. According to US studies, 70 percent of all people under the age of 35 have their mobile phone near their beds when they sleep. More than half checks new messages when waking up at night.[9]

At the same time, the younger generation has also socially differentiated its digital communication channels. Only very few of them can manage without WhatsApp. But there are firm rules of etiquette. In making appointments, answers should be sent within 20 to 30 minutes. Other messages can remain unanswered for a day or two. Some people even make regular dates to chat – in most cases to maintain contact over long distances. Even though the number of their acquaintances is much higher, Gen Zers mainly communicate regularly with close friends.

Although Nicolas did delete his Instagram account, he has never managed to do without Snapchat. He explains that he has many friends who live elsewhere. He could also contact them via WhatsApp, of course, "But if you write on WhatsApp, you always end up in longer conversations," he says. "With Snapchat…" he starts explaining and suddenly stops to ask his (Gen X) interviewer, "Do you know anything about Snapchat at all…?"

Snapchat seems to be *the* network that divides the generations as otherwise only TikTok could. Launched in California's Silicon Valley as a social network that deletes any information posted within 24 hours – so as to avoid last year's awkward hair cut from popping up again and again – Snapchat is aimed at young people in search of a space outside of their parents' control. Legend has it that the functionalities of the network were deliberately designed to be more complicated than necessary to keep parents away.

"You can always ask people quick things, like how they're doing," explains Nicolas. "I think that's pretty cool." It is the time limit that makes the difference. "You can send just a picture, and there's only room for a short message." Snapchat has thus become the postcard of Generation Z.

Even compared to its direct predecessor (Generation Y, currently between 20 and 35), Generation Z seems to be much more pragmatic in dealing with the online world. For them, technical innovations are supposed to make their life easier, possibly enrich it, but definitely not control it. While Generation Y was still enthusiastic about any new technology and often drifted through the digital world, Generation Z seems more mellow and self-assured. They handle social networks naturally, but essentially only see them as a useful starting point for their contacts.

Facebook has long been out of fashion. "I never used Facebook," says 14-year-old Tida, who is in grade 9 at a secondary school in Giessen. Then she adds, "I don't even know exactly what it looks like." While Facebook has become the epitome of online activity for many older people – it is, after all, the largest global social network– it is an unknown world for some digital natives.

Instead, Instagram and Snapchat – in addition to WhatsApp and YouTube – are on almost every smartphone belonging to the younger generation. Here, far away from parental control, Generation Z maintains their friendships in the digital world. Gen Zers counter the dominance of Facebook with diversity; many of them belong to nine different networks and are active on five or six of them. Some use the word processing software Google Docs to chat, others the game app Clash of Clans.

"This behaviour is currently the most effective means of counteracting digital monopolies," writes Sascha Lobo. "It significantly reduces the dependence on individual digital companies."[10] In Germany, the younger generation also uses different social networks for different purposes: TikTok for funny music videos, Instagram to follow famous people and Snapchat to communicate with friends. This has also become another way to counteract digital monopolies – until those networks are bought up by Facebook, as has already happened with Instagram and WhatsApp.

Generation Z wants an open internet free from state and corporate surveillance. At the beginning of 2019, the European Union enacted a reform of copyright law. Article 13 aimed to limit the sharing of copyrighted material by putting pressure on platforms like YouTube to monitor content. Young people in particular feared that the platforms would apply restrictive content filters that would stifle creativity. Youth were thus especially prominent in the protests against the EU directive.

At the same time, Generation Z is committed to effective data protection. Although 16-year-old Ben feels he cannot do without WhatsApp, he communicates via Signal whenever possible, a secure messenger service recommended by Edward Snowden, the whistle-blower who exposed the US National Security Agency's large-scale data collection.

Scepticism about the current lack of data protection has increased in recent years, especially among girls who are more critical on this issue than their male peers. When it comes to the question "What happens to my data?" the carefree attitude of older generations is gone. It might only be a matter of time until a critical movement will emerge to keep the internet free. Maybe it will once again be a female voice that rises up and makes her generation take to the streets, as Greta Thunberg did for the climate crisis: Young women are already slightly more active online today (93 percent) than men (90 percent) and use the internet much more for communication (41 to 30 percent).[11]

Traditional media in a downward spiral

Monday morning at the secondary school in Giessen. Class 9c discusses how they can find information about the climate crisis, as well as world events. "From the newspaper," says the first student. "And from the Tagesschau." "From the Tagesschau," repeats a second student. The Tagesschau is Germany's most popular evening news programme; it runs on public television. When the third student mentions the Tagesschau, it comes to a vote. Only two or three out of 27 students do not watch the news programme regularly.

And yet classic television has gone completely out of fashion. According to polls, young people hardly ever pick up a printed newspaper and they watch TV only now and then with their parents. Their most important political information channels are online: News websites, including those of paper newspapers, news portals and push notifications, including those put out by television stations. They want to decide for themselves when and where they watch films, videos and the news – and with which devices. As a rule, the smartphone is their device of choice. Even public broadcasters in Germany are now seriously considering whether they need to be present on TikTok.

Most Gen Zers are not used to searching for political information. They want to read the news on the side while on their networks. Only 37 percent say they take active steps to inform themselves about current events. They prefer to receive the news on their smartphones. Public service broadcasting aimed at Generation Z should be fun, but also be serious. The Tagesschau – as Germany's most important news programme – has over one million followers on Instagram, Gen Z's favourite social network.[12]

Generation Z is growing up in a time in which the leadership of the traditional media has increasingly been called into question. A growing number of citizens state that they have little or no trust in the media. The most common reasons are worries about deliberate manipulation or bias. But even if young people are increasingly turning away from traditional forms of media such as television and printed newspapers and are spending a lot of time on YouTube and the like, they still trust the big brands. In Germany, most young people believe that the television news shows produced by the major public broadcasters are trustworthy. The figures for the major national daily newspapers are similar. On the opposite side of the spectrum, only seven percent rate information YouTube as "very trustworthy"; overall, less than 50 percent trust what they see on the video platform. Facebook and Twitter perform even worse: Two thirds of young people consider the information on these platforms to be barely trustworthy or completely untrustworthy.[13]

This means that Gen Z may be less susceptible to fake news than their parents and grandparents. A study out of Princeton University looked at who actually shares fake news, by zeroing in on the 2016 US presidential election. "On average, users over 65 shared nearly seven times as many articles from fake news domains as the youngest age group," defined here as 18 to 29-year-olds.[14] One possible explanation for this discrepancy is young people's trust in the major media outlets. In the UK and the US, these are brands like the BBC, *The Guardian* or *The New York Times*. In Germany, it is invariably the public broadcasters, ARD (which broadcasts the Tagesschau) and ZDF. That is why class 9c in Giessen watches Tagesschau.

YouTube – a parallel universe?

"Yes, it's time for another one of those videos" is how Rezo opens his newest YouTube video on 18 May 2019. The 27-year-old with blue hair has been running two channels on the video platform for four years, with a total of two million subscribers. He and his team looked into the party platform of the conservative, governing CDU, Rezo says. "And I have to say honestly, fuck, this is bad," he adds.

Orange hoodie, baseball cap, several guitars leaning against the wall in the background – it is not quite clear from the video whether Rezo is broadcasting from his bedroom at his parents' or an office. "In this video I'll show how the CDU lies, how it lacks basic competence for the job, how it makes policy that clearly goes against expert opinions, [...] how it uses propaganda and lies against the young generation."[15] "The destruction of the CDU" remains online today; it is a meticulous one-hour analysis of the politics of Angela Merkel's party; and shook up not only Germany's governing party, but also the European elections that took place one week later. Rezo originally became famous for his music parodies. Then he started commenting on political issues. His rant against Germany's conservative party is accompanied by a link to a document with 13 pages of sources and evidence. "You know that whenever I make a video, I do it properly." Social justice, education, climate, defence. It is a no-holds-barred ride through a decade of German politics, a fundamental critique of the Merkel era. "It's not because I am actively trying to destroy someone," Rezo says at the beginning of the video, "but because the facts and figures simply show that the CDU is destroying itself, its reputation and its election results."

In many ways, the video is typical of the political thinking of the younger generation. Rezo argues based on facts and then draws clear conclusions. There is no ideological argumentation around principles but instead an evaluation and categorisation of complex issues. Some of them could certainly be interpreted differently, but his arguments are still based on verifiable facts. Politics is thus no longer a question of ideology or convictions, but a search for solutions and an optimisation of possible benefits.

Rezo is well aware of his generation's weak position in German politics. He knows that his – mostly younger – audience will not be able to tilt elections on their own, which is why he called on them to carry his message to the older generations. After all, they determine the outcome of the elections in Germany. Rezo managed to make a rather rational expert discussion based on facts appear attractive and sent a thoroughly democratic message. After millions of young YouTube users clicked on "The Destruction of the CDU," major media outlets were forced to report on the video.

For the CDU, however, the video – just days away from the European elections – was so unsettling that their only response was stunned silence. The party had no strategy whatsoever for dealing with something like this. A video response by Philipp Amthor, the youngest member of the CDU parliamentary group known for acting far older than his actual age and defending positions wildly out of step with his own generation, was recorded and then never released. Instead, a factsheet was published – eleven pages as a pdf document.

Traditional parties like the CDU and SPD are struggling with social media. Establishing relevant communities, addressing and mobilising specific target groups, setting the digital agenda are still huge challenges for them, though they are the governing parties.

A look at Russia reveals the huge political potential of platforms like YouTube. For years, the Kremlin has been building a propaganda machine which allows them to carry their messages to the most remote parts of the country. State television is at the centre of the strategy, as it remains the country's most important and accessible medium. When, a couple of years ago, student protests against President Vladimir Putin took the Kremlin by surprise, it became clear that Putin's regime had lost control over a demographic that knew state television only from visiting their grandparents. Instead, they watched YouTube and Co., where the Kremlin had much less influence. Even worse: Building up authentic YouTubers with Putin-friendly messages proved a major challenge for the Kremlin. While YouTube is still the land of make-up tutorials and music videos, young people clearly also use the platform – despite often restrictive government policies – to create new public spaces and engage in necessary political speech and dialogue.

In our ageing societies that are dominated by older cohorts, Gen Z makes their voices heard by creating their own public sphere. Online, the young generation has started a conversation about the state of our society. It uses the internet to organise and coordinate their activism. While weaker groups struggle with the potential for distraction and addiction the online world offers, the well-educated among Zers enter this debate better-informed than their predecessors, having the necessary competencies to make use of the vast resources the internet offers. Many debates stay under the radar of mainstream society. However, as shown by Rezo's example, once they surface, they have the power to make an impact. Thus, they pose a challenge to authorities, but also to the older generations as a whole.

As the digital sphere provides Gen Z with a platform to have their say about the future, they will continue to fight for a free internet that works for everyone, not just for companies like Facebook or Google. Society should listen to what they have to say while schools need to make sure that all parts of Generation Z acquire the competencies to use the internet for their own benefit.

Notes

1 Lobo 2019, p. 386.
2 Children's Commissioner 2018.
3 Pereira et al. 2020.

4 Wolfert and Leven 2019, p. 214.
5 SZ 2019.
6 Wolfert and Leven 2019, p. 237.
7 mpfs 2018, p. 60.
8 Stiglic and Viner 2019
9 Seemiller and Grace 2019.
10 Lobo 2019, p. 375.
11 mpfs 2020, p. 31 ff.
12 Schneekloth and Albert 2019, p. 53.
13 Wolfert and Leven 2019, p. 243.
14 Guess et al. 2019.
15 Rezo 2019.

Chapter 7

Interactive education
Demand for more digitalisation at school

Even digital natives need digital skills

In 2019, a cartoon in the *The New Yorker* showed a mother sitting at home in her study. On the desk in front of her, an open laptop; next to her, her little daughter, hardly tall enough to peek over the tabletop. The mother reaches out to her daughter almost pleadingly. A generation ago, the mother's wide-open and the downturned mouth would have been interpreted as an invitation for physical contact. Instead, the little girl with the cute ribbon in her hair is completely confused. "You want to cuddle?" she asks almost indignantly. "I thought you needed help with the computer."

As digital natives, Gen Zers grew up with digital technology. And they certainly appreciate it. Sixty-two percent of young people in Germany believe that digitalisation offers more advantages than disadvantages. Only 5 percent are sceptical. At the same time, this generation is well aware of the challenges of living online. When asked what schools should teach in addition to the classical subjects, the second most important topic was the use of computer programmes (72 percent), and 63 percent also wanted to learn more about the responsible use of social networks, personal data and apps.[1] Only 18 percent of those surveyed feel sufficiently supported both in their use of social networks and in the protection of their data. "I feel like there should be more warnings about all the things that can happen online, what one should be on the look-out for, and what all the possible risks are," says Joy from Bielefeld. Here, the 16-year-old is thinking not only about viruses and data theft, but also the x-rated videos that circulate in WhatsApp groups without user consent.

In many schools, however, there is still plenty of room for improvement. Long before the school closures due to the coronavirus pandemic, students criticised the lack of digital learning in their classrooms. Rightfully so, as the majority of schools in Germany continue to struggle to manage the transition from analogue to digital. Only about one fourth of all schools, mostly pre-university secondary schools, had the hardware and software to provide professional remote teaching and maintain ongoing contact with students outside of school.

In Germany, students are allocated to two different types of secondary schools according to their performance level after only four years of elementary school. *Gymnasium* is the most attractive because it offers the longest schooling period and provides students with an *Abitur* after 12 or 13 years (depending on the federal state and the student's educational biography), paving the path to university (although it can also be used for all other types of further education). Almost 50 percent of students attend Gymnasium, and their number has increased dramatically in recent decades. Apart from Gymnasium schools, there are *Sekundarschulen* – schools which originally only offered a basic qualification after nine years and an intermediate qualification after ten years of schooling. More and more of these schools have subsequently introduced a pre-university stream (*Gymnasiale Oberstufe*) that allows them to prepare students for the Abitur.

Despite all the inequalities the German educational system produces, the Abitur as the sole entry requirement for university constitutes a stark difference from the UK. Germany's universities accept students on the basis of their Abitur. The grades count only in highly popular disciplines with more applicants than capacity.

The fact that Germany's school system sets its pupils on an educational track at the age of ten already means it reproduces existing inequalities at this early age. In the UK, with its system of state schools, grammar schools and private education, it is the transition to higher education that is especially problematic. In 2018, 63 percent of private-school students achieved an A (or grade seven or above) in their GCSEs compared with a national average of 23 percent, write Francis Green and David Kynaston, authors of the book *Engines of Privilege: Britain's Private School Problem*.

> Perhaps inevitably, by far the highest-profile stats concern Oxbridge, where between 2010 and 2015 an average of 43% of offers from Oxford and 37% from Cambridge were made to privately educated students, and there has been no sign since of any significant opening up.[2]

At the same time, only one in every 16 pupils attends a private-school.

Germany does not know such a system of elite education. Most of its private schools are run by the church, but still funded by the state, levelling the importance of the school attended as long as it leads to the Abitur. And while some universities receive additional funding for scientific or academic excellence, the country lacks any institution that compares even remotely to Oxford or Cambridge.

Joy is about to graduate from one of Bielefeld's Sekundarschulen with her intermediate qualification. She likes the friendly relationship between teachers and students at school. "What I don't like is that some important learning tools are missing – like laptops." The latter were usually damaged when needed, she says. "IT lessons are a must nowadays," adds her friend Nino. "These days, so much more is run virtually," says Joy in November 2019, four months before the pandemic hit Germany. "You could [theoretically] also bring your own laptop and then send the homework directly to the teacher." Joy imagines a school in which the teacher could then correct and grade her homework before sending it back again. "I find that much easier and much better." And it also makes the lessons more interesting. "This way the teacher doesn't need to write everything on the board."

This is already the case in Berlin-Schöneberg. Sophie Scholl Secondary School has already entered the digital age. When Christoph Köhn, an English teacher, wants to turn the page of the textbook, he clicks on the upper left corner of the smartboard (a digital board with a touch screen); a few more clicks and he finds the exercise he is looking for. With a digital pen, he writes the solutions directly into the text. At the end, his writing disappears again with a single click. No one has wiped the board here in a long time.

"Education and digitalisation" are the most important political issues for Kurt, the Social Democratic party youth organisation member campaigning in Eberswalde. "For us, this was the classic fight," the 19-year-old recalls from his school days. "We wanted free Wi-Fi for everyone, so that you could take your laptop with you and work with it at school." Since 2018, the federal government has provided support to the 16 federal states (which are solely responsible for education policy in Germany) with a *DigitalPakt* allocating an additional 5.5 billion euros for hardware and software upgrades in German schools. An additional one million euros were made available during the coronavirus pandemic to support students and teachers with laptops. But progress is slow. "I don't see that anything has changed at my school over the past five years," Kurt observes.

When it comes to digital learning, Germany is far behind most other European countries. In 2018, three quarters of students in Germany studied in schools without Wi-Fi access, according to the results of the 2018 International Computer and Information Literacy Study (ICILS).[3] It is the poorest result of the 12 participating industrialised nations. In countries such as Denmark, Finland and Portugal, Wi-Fi access is close to 100 percent. Where no Wi-Fi connection is available, students in Germany use their mobile data, even as the poorer among them quickly reach the limits of their data plan.

Schools and teachers in Germany are on the verge of losing their pedagogical authority as they fail to respond to the real challenges faced by young people in their everyday lives. Generation Z has noticed that their schools' timetables lack certain topics they consider vital. They are unhappy not only with the teaching methodologies on offer, but, in particular, with the training in media and information literacy they receive, which is critical for the kind of life-long learning that awaits Generation Z after they finish school. Theoretically, young people have unlimited access to knowledge and disinformation alike, and their future success will depend heavily on their ability to judge the quality and accuracy of information.

For that reason, the younger generation has begun to demand that their teachers and schools better prepare them for the digital future than they are currently able to. Before the coronavirus pandemic, 41 percent of young people rated the digital competence of their teachers negatively.[4]

Even for progressive schools, digitalisation remains an enormous challenge. "We first have to acquire the knowledge ourselves," says Juliane Westphal, the head teacher at Sophie Scholl Secondary School in Berlin. "And then we're supposed to teach it to the students in a critical way." At the same time, technology develops so fast it is hard to keep up. "And the third thing is that we should prepare them for a work environment in which they are expected to be proficient in using this technology. This places incredibly high demands on the educational system," says the head teacher. "I would like to have some support here, but there isn't any."

In contrast to the subjects they were trained (and hired) to teach, most teachers are neither trained experts in media and information literacy, nor do they have the time to acquire the necessary skills. The rapid development of computers, smartphones and their applications requires a constant training and re-training process. Unfortunately, Germany's 16 federal states still have no programme in place to address this issue or to systematically offer skills training to their teachers.

There is, however, a policy paper on "education in the digital world" negotiated by the federal states in 2016. According to this white paper, teaching and school life should provide the maximum range of skills required for active and self-determined participation in the digital world. Digital literacy should be an integral part of all subjects and teach the most important skills necessary for dealing with information online: searching for, processing and storing information; communicating and cooperating safely and smartly; producing and presenting online; digital self-protection and safe engagement; problem-solving, analysing and reflecting.

The joint recommendations of the 16 federal states are characterised by efforts to strengthen the existing phalanx of subjects without introducing any new ones. In a rapidly changing world, however, this approach is obviously insufficient. Students lack work-related skills in using smartphones and computers. These skills cannot be taught in history or geography class. Schools need to offer a new course in "media and information literacy." This new subject, which has already proved successful in several experimental schools, focuses on creative and critical learning. Students have to assess the quality of information independently, link knowledge from different sources and apply it in concrete situations, thereby teaching them to shape their own ways of learning beyond the boundaries of school.

Finally, the school curriculum must also include an additional course in computer science with a focus on robotics and artificial intelligence. Thus far, such a class has only been implemented at a few particularly ambitious schools.

It was only under the shock of the coronavirus pandemic that some momentum was gained on the digital front. In March 2020, schools were forced to close, practically overnight, and switch from face-to-face to distance learning. Only 25 percent of schools – those that were already engaged in digital learning, such as Sophie Scholl School in Berlin – managed to do so without major problems. Most other schools experienced enormous difficulties in maintaining contact with the students and their parents. In short: The pandemic was a massive wake-up call that jolted most teachers from their digital slumber. Since then, education ministers and school principals across the country have tried to get a hold on the situation.

Beyond proper equipment and platforms, all schools need to provide both advanced training for their staff and specialists for the installation, care and maintenance of Wi-Fi networks, computers and tablets. In addition, IT experts must support teachers in the classroom. In a class of 30 students, teachers reach their physical limits when the software fails for even just a few of them. "Technology quickly eats away at the teaching plan," says one teacher.

Mobile phones at school

Julia is about to graduate with an Abitur from a pre-university secondary school in a wealthy Berlin suburb. There is, however, one battle she still wants to win before graduation. Until now, the entirety of the school grounds is a mobile-free zone: The school's rulebook states that only a switched-off phone is a good phone. For Julia and her classmates, this rule ignores the reality of their lives. "Smartphones have long been part of professional and everyday lives," she says. "If you don't learn how to use it at school, you have less chances of dealing with it in a reasonable way later on."

Julia's school is definitely pro-tech. She uses school laptops regularly in class, including the GeoGebra programme in maths class or for researching and writing essays in other subjects. Far too often, she faces problems logging on to the school server. "But if that works, the laptop really helps."

Considering how technologically savvy the school is when it comes to computers, the more its stance on smartphones seems straight from the stone age in Julia's view. "Right now, we need to leave school grounds to Google something," Julia says. A ridiculous situation. After all, even teachers sometimes do not know the answer to certain questions. "At the moment, they're forced to say, 'Google that at home.'"

Which is why the students want to change the rules. Their proposal, submitted to the school council: "Smartphones should generally be allowed, but they have to be in flight mode or switched off during lessons," except when teachers decide to actively use them with their students in class. Older students could then at least go online during breaks in their schedule.

Julia and her classmates are well aware of the dangers that smartphones carry at school. Even under their proposed new rules, anyone who bullies classmates online or makes video recordings in class must be prepared to have their mobile phone confiscated by the school administration. However, she does not think that students are in any danger of completely drowning in the virtual world during breaks. "We know how to put our phones aside," says Julia. They regularly do it after school anyway.

Most federal states leave it to the schools themselves to set the rules for digital devices, leaving open the possibility for conflict across the country's educational systems. Rosenhöhe Secondary School in Bielefeld has opted for the strictest solution: Anyone caught looking at their smartphone must say goodbye to it for two weeks – unless a parent makes the effort to pick it up from the school administration for them. Tom is really annoyed by this rule. "We have an hour for lunch." While there are activities for the younger ones, "we only chill for an hour. And then you're not even allowed to pick up the phone and write your friends." Listening to music is forbidden, as well. "Not even that."

In a Giessen secondary school, teachers can grant their students access to the school's Wi-Fi network in order to allow them to use their mobile phones in class. At all other times, phones must be put away. Students report that not everyone complies with this rule.

School as a phone-free zone – what a contrast to the real world! Today, 95 percent of 12-year-olds have their own smartphone. And for most of them, it is by no means just a toy. The younger generation also sees mobile phones as work tools. They look things up, watch educational films on YouTube or use their phones as a calculator.

Anyone who studied physics in the pre-digital era was used to consulting a second or third textbook to fully understand a subject. Carla, who is about to get her Abitur in Frankfurt an der Oder, watches YouTube clips when she does not fully understand something like photosynthesis in her biology class. "It's better to have things explained differently," says the 16-year-old. "I can also remember the material better when I see it. That's why I use my phone to study." The rest of the time, she tries to put her mobile away when she needs to concentrate.

"We use our mobiles to do research on the internet when we need something for school," says 13-year-old Lennart from Sophie Scholl School in Berlin-Schöneberg. His German teacher recently set up a quiz on the Kahoot! platform. "Then everybody in the group gets out their mobile phones and logs on to the website," Lennart explains. "You get points for speed and for correct answers."

At Julia's school in the Berlin suburbs, the students' initiative to allow phones on the school territory sparked weeks of discussion. In the end, the school administrators remained unconvinced by the proposal and rejected it. Only after graduation will Julia be able to decide for herself when her mobile phone is switched on.

Digitally native swipers

On Wednesdays before fifth period starts, head teacher Juliane Westphal loads a box of tablets onto a small cart and pushes it to the elevator that will take her to the fourth floor. Seventh-graders Jana and Luisa attend Frau Westphal's class. While half of the class learns a second foreign language, the other half receives extra German instruction. Together with almost a dozen other students whose grades were not high enough to sign up for a second foreign language, they are catching up instead: six weeks of German, six weeks of English and six weeks of maths.

Using the tablets, the students are putting together PowerPoint presentations for German class about the book *In the Sea There Are Crocodiles* by Fabio Geda. In their presentation, they recount the story of 10-year-old Enaiatollah and his flight to Europe. "It's about a boy who is abandoned by his mother," says Jana. "There's a war going on, and so the two of them flee. But then, the mother returns to the country they are fleeing from and leaves the boy alone." Lien and her classmate Luisa like the story. Each of them has to describe one part of the flight with a PowerPoint presentation.

Thus, a dozen seventh-grade students sit with their tablets, switching between Word, PowerPoint and the internet. "Many of them struggle to determine what information actually belongs on a slide," says Westphal. This is exactly the goal of the project: learning to evaluate and process information correctly.

The head teacher, however, faces very different challenges with the remedial German class. Although the students are supposed to work independently on their presentations, during the lesson there are as many hands waving in the air as there are working on the tablets. Some of their questions, including "How do I copy and paste my text from the Word document into the PowerPoint presentation?" raise serious doubts about the often repeated dictum of the younger generation as digital natives.

"The students are digital natives only when it comes to swiping on their screens," Westphal says. Many of them have a good eye for optics, such as how a background image will appear on a slide, she says. But beyond that, they are extremely passive in their use of technology.

Only a small percentage of Generation Z is proficient with digital technology, with one in five admitting that they feel overwhelmed by technology and content creation. Some of the written texts Westphal receives when she asks her grade seven students to assess their learning capabilities with the help of a learning programme are completely incomprehensible, even when typed out on the keyboard. "I think that the children believe that when they type something into the computer, the computer corrects it; that there's a kind of autocorrect that corrects spelling, punctuation, and probably even sentence structure and content."

There is also a lot of banging around on the keyboard. Westphal observes that a large share of the information on the screen often goes ignored. Their use of computers reminds her of being on social networks such as Snapchat or Instagram, which are geared towards entertainment, consumption and distraction. "But they have no idea that a computer is a functional medium or what it can offer."

Despite having grown up with digital technology, only a few in Generation Z are able to use it competently. Skills such as simple pro- gramming, the sensible use of smartphones and computers, and an awareness of the dangers of the internet need to become a part of a basic education, lest some students get left behind.

According to the ICILS survey, teachers in Germany use digital media the least in their daily classes compared to the other 11 participating countries.[5] It is thus almost surprising that students' media skills are still average in international comparisons. They have apparently learned to complete assignments with the help of a computer from family and friends. However, every third eighth-grade student possesses only rudimentary computer skills, such as how to open a link in a new tab. They lack the ability to layout texts, research online or produce content themselves. Schools are systematically failing at training students in these skills.

To meet this objective, the Sophie Scholl School has become certified as a test centre for the European Computer Driving Licence. Students have to acquire basic knowledge in Word, Excel and the internet, according to Juliane Westphal, the head teacher: "What's a spreadsheet? What can I really do with Word, besides bang around on a keyboard? What else can this amazing programme do?"

For Westphal, digital tools will always remain a means to an end; they will never replace lessons. She has never seriously considered switching to so-called tablet classes, which rely solely on digital learning. "I believe that the computer is a tool to make things more efficient, but you first have to be able to understand these things cognitively and also be able to do them in an analogue way [before jumping to digital]."

As important as it is to be able to operate digital programmes, technology also limits creativity and critical thinking. "Tablet kids are at the complete mercy of those who do the programming," Westphal points out. "This teaches them a consumer behaviour that doesn't help them in the long run." Acquiring programming skills for later first means being able to think beyond existing applications – something that is still best done with paper and pen.

Interactive school

Madeleine and Julie, grade 10 students at the Sophie Scholl School, get more and more excited as they discuss a United Nations simulation game they played as part of their political science class. The game deals with small farmers who have lost their land to agribusinesses. "There were different actors," says Madeleine. "The government, the United Nations, the agribusinesses and the small farmers. And we tried to come up with a solution." In small groups, the students developed the positions of the individual actors. "We worked on this for a long time," Julie recalls. "Everybody got involved."

While similar conflicts exist in many countries of the Global South, such tensions have also developed in rich European countries, when it comes to construction mega-projects like high-speed railway lines or new wind parks. "I learned that it's totally complicated to find political and social solutions," Madeleine says. "Everyone has a different viewpoint," Julie adds. "Everyone wants to achieve something else." What sticks is a basic understanding of how the reconciliation of interests works in politics. "I played the United Nations," Madeleine recalls. "I realised that it's really, really complicated as an impartial party to find a decision that doesn't negatively affect anyone," she says and grins a little at the verbiage of the "impartial party." When you watch the news, you often wonder how politicians can make such crazy decisions on issues like Brexit, she says. "But I think once you're the one confronted with the problem, it's not so easy anymore."

In divisive political times, when populist parties succeed at the polls, this kind of deeper understanding of the nature of political decision-making is much more important than merely knowing the facts – those can always be Googled.

Digitalisation has changed the requirements in the working world for how people acquire, evaluate and deploy information; those best able to consider how information is embedded in specific contexts, patterns and communities and then categorise that newfound knowledge are the ones most likely to succeed. More important than the information itself is knowing where to find it, how to assess it and then how to apply it.

In this new world, the traditional role of teachers as suppliers and disseminators of knowledge is no longer sufficient. Students must learn to access and acquire knowledge on their own, while teachers need to act as trainers who set learning objectives, assign tasks and jointly evaluate the results. However, much as with football training, they often only intervene in order to help correct mistakes. Gen Z wants an interactive learning experience worthy of the digital age. They want to explore topics themselves instead of following a strict lesson plan. Thus, students want to actively determine their own pace in groups or pairs and, to a certain extent, set the level of difficulty. Instead of simply obeying the teacher's instructions, Gen Z students value individual support tailored to them and their abilities, while still allowing them to take the initiative themselves. Especially the smart ones know that success depends on close cooperation with teachers and that their education is a process of co-production: They want to learn interactively.

Vodafone Foundation Germany recently presented the German Teacher Award in the category "Innovative Teaching" to a mathematics project in which the teachers divided lesson content among themselves and recorded it. The unique thing about it? The video clips were used outside the classroom. The students studied the material at home, for example how the rule of three works, and then applied what they had learned in class – which also allowed them to receive help from the teacher or their peers.

This concept, "flipping the classroom," has literally turned the traditional classroom model upside down. The successful completion of maths homework no longer depends on whether Mum or Dad can help at home, since students do their homework at school with the teacher. Digital technology can thus help reduce educational inequality.

Another approach to interactive learning is project work, which is highly valued at the secondary school in Giessen. According to Sandra Sudler, one of the school's main objectives is for students to acquire the ability to work independently, which is why she as a teacher frequently organises learning stations in the classroom or integrates project phases into the lesson plan.

For a project on the Middle Ages, Karl, Nele and Celina developed a shadow play. They wrote the dialogues, constructed a stage and the figures and performed the piece. For another project on newspapers, teens conducted research for a report on single parents. The final result is that students learn to learn. Many of them work independently on difficult material and set up their own plan of action.

For a majority of the younger generation, interactive learning fulfils the desire for individual self-determination. Most young people understand that, as digital natives, they can Google information anytime, which is why – just like Madeleine and Julie with the UN simulation – they are much more interested in processes and contexts, aspects which Wikipedia or YouTube tutorials do not adequately convey. Computers, smartphones and gaming have taught them how to plan a project independently, step-by-step, and to then ask for clear instructions on how to proceed further. They value teachers for their expert guidance, while taking control of their own learning.

"It depends a lot on how the teacher organises the lessons," says 13-year-old Lennart. "When all we do is memorise stuff, it's a little boring. But when we play games, then it's fun." Lennart just read a short story in English class about two American teens, who, on the way back from basketball training, are stopped by the police. After reading the story, the students developed a role-play in small groups. Lennart played Lance, the Black driver of the car. In the story, Lance is convinced that he has been stopped only because of the colour of his skin. Lennart feels motivated by this way of teaching: "When you play games and it's fun, you also want to learn something." Charlotte, one of his classmates, likes working with a partner and thinks working alone is dumb. "It's more fun together."

Interactive learning poses huge challenges for teachers. It means acquiring new techniques and might include learning how to handle digital devices in a classroom setting; it also means developing a new understanding of their role as the teacher – part of a larger shift in how authority is expressed in society and in working life. In the wake of greater individualisation and digital change, the old model of a manager giving top-down instructions has retreated in favour of team leaders on par with their teams. Similarly, the role of teachers is moving toward that of the moderator, coordinator, facilitator or trainer.

"Good mor-ning, Mr Pie-kar-ski!" the 22 tenth-grade students mechanically drone out the daily greeting at the start of the political science class. Despite this seemingly old-fashioned ritual, there is no sign of passivity here at Sophie Scholl School. Gentrification is currently on the lesson plan – an issue that is literally graffitied on the building walls everywhere in Berlin. From their own doorsteps, every student in the class has been able to observe how their neighbourhood has changed in recent years. In class, they are now able to learn about how the spiral of rising rents, evictions and displacement is set off.

At the end of the unit, Mr Piekarski, the political science teacher, plays a documentary, *Who Owns This City?*, which sheds light on the phenomenon through developments in the Berlin district of Prenzlauer Berg. In the discussion that follows, Piekarski is free to call on anyone in class; everyone has something to add to the discussion.

"Cities shouldn't allow gentrification in every district," argues Henriette. Her classmate thinks that it is just tough luck if someone cannot afford to live in a certain area. Henriette, however, sees the long arm of twenty-first century capitalism at work. "The powerful, those with more money, win," she states and adds, "But gentrification also leads to modernisation." It is a difficult question, the classmate sitting next to her admits. Of course, long-time residents shouldn't feel as if they are being driven away, "but newcomers also have the right to live there so that the city can continue to develop."

The enthusiastic debate is Piekarski's reward for several weeks of inter-active lessons that included giving students the freedom to develop their own understanding of the topic. On the basis of articles and working together in pairs, they independently worked out the problems but also the positive effects of gentrification. Working in small groups, they then drew up charts which plotted the individual phases of development – from the arrival of the first newcomers, usually students, to districts with cheap rent and many empty apartments to hyper-gentrification. Following the class discussion of the film, they brainstorm political solutions which could help curb evictions before heading to the computer lab to research what the city and civil society are already doing to counteract the negative consequences of gentrification.

Piekarski's role is no longer that of a traditional teacher, but he remains responsible for shaping the core structure of the class. This includes the ability to assess what his students are expected to accomplish, to determine who runs the risk of becoming overwhelmed and offer help where it is needed. His authority is no longer based purely on knowing more about the subject than his students, but also on teaching them how to acquire knowledge in general: How is it generated, checked, classified, applied and transferred to a given situation?

Such interactive teaching is by no means the rule in German schools. "Everything's evolving, technology included, but school still looks just like the pictures from 100 years ago," says Nino from Rosenhöhe Secondary School in Bielefeld. The school puts a strong emphasis on interactive learning as well. Nevertheless, Nino dreams of a school that allows her even more freedom. "I think that much more attention should be paid to individual people and their strengths," Nino says. "So that you have the chance to develop what you're good at and learn what you need to work on at the same time." Nino would like more science classes, but only two hours of physics are offered per week. "Here, everyone gets lumped together, it's a one-size-fits all approach."

This outdated school system is creating friction between Gen Zers and their elders. As with the political system, many have the impression that their schools are trapped in rigid structures born of a previous century. This remains true not only for the material taught in their classrooms, but also for the processes that guide the school day, from the mechanical rhythm of the bell to the chopped-up daily schedule, which makes diving deep into a single topic for a project assignment difficult and unsatisfying.

Notes

1 Köcher et al. 2019, p. 52.
2 Green and Kynaston 2019.
3 Fraillon et al. 2019, p. 43.
4 Köcher et al. 2019, p. 55.
5 Fraillon et al. 2019, p. 121.

Chapter 8

What schools lack

Developing knowledge and skills for life

School companies

"The year is 2009, Schöneberg has been explored and charted, and only one small speck of earth remains to be cultivated," writes Lukas, who is in tenth grade at Sophie Scholl Secondary School. "And then one day, Mr K. from the economics, technology and labour class comes along and goes to work on this little patch of weeds." Lukas is describing is the founding story of the school's "green classroom" in Berlin-Schöneberg.

Ten years later, the school is collecting donations on Betterplace.org for what used to be called a school garden, which – if Lukas is to be believed – consisted mainly of thicket. The school wants to expand the green classroom and needs approximately 1,000 euros for a professional greenhouse and a digital irrigation system. The crowdfunding video shows a small garden with winding paths in the courtyard of the old, dignified school building. Logs heat a clay oven while students dissect plants outdoors under a microscope. There is even a beehive.

The video summarises the concept of the green classroom:

> In a world in which their actual production has become more and more obscured by high-tech systems, it is all the more important to reproduce the gigantic span of food production on a small scale and in an educational way to increase the visibility of the connections between ecology and the economy.

To this end, school-based student companies are to be established based on the urban gardening project.

Student companies are a hands-on pedagogical concept: With the support of their teachers, students set up a real company and learn the basics of economic activity. The green classroom focuses on ecological interrelationships and a more sustainable economy, which allows the school to work through parts of the curriculum and – at the same time – prepare students for the working world. It turns Gen Z into responsible citizens who can critically engage with the economic system.

At other schools, school companies offer computer courses to senior citizens, run a travel agency for students and teachers, arrange tutoring or run the cafeteria or the media centre. Thus, students learn intuitively about supply and demand, competition and market structure, client and customer care and social justice in the distribution of scarce resources.

From a pedagogical point of view, a student company works like an interdisciplinary project that systematically links different subjects and curriculum units. The focus is on key economic issues, such as the distribution of scarce resources or the efficient use of capital and labour. Questions concerning the calculation of costs and revenues are dealt with during maths class, for example, while in German class, students write the text for their company's webpage. A unit in political science class addresses the effects of globalisation in terms of the relocation of production sites to low-wage countries, as well as the influence of large international corporations on agricultural production and working conditions in the wake of automation and digitalisation. Thus, in a sense, the school garden at Sophie Scholl Secondary School becomes a version of the world in miniature.

A school for life

Generation Z is growing up at a time when schools as institutions seek answers to social and technological change. The school closures during the initial phase of the coronavirus pandemic have intensified the conversation surrounding these issues. In recent years, young people have faced increasing challenges, as the emphasis has shifted from simply completing a school-leaving certificate as a means of getting a good job one day to having to pass assessments that also test soft skills such as interpersonal skills, stress management and teamwork. Young people want more support from their schools; when asked what schools should teach beyond the classical subjects, they focus on skills that prepare them for life.[1]

Most young people want lessons that prepare them for the real world in the digital age. They want teachers who can communicate competently and enable learning on an equal footing. They do not question the importance of existing school subjects but nevertheless think a classical education is no longer sufficient. Instead they want to add networking, effective money management, media and information literacy, sustainable consumer behaviour and even political engagement to the curriculum.

Leo goes to a secondary school in Giessen which places a heavy emphasis on projects and integrates much more practical learning into the lesson plan than classical forward-facing (teacher-centred) learning allows. But he is still not satisfied. He is interested in politics and the influence of lobbyists on political decision-making. For three quarters of an hour, he patiently discusses Fridays for Future, YouTubers, politicians and how he uses his smartphone.

After answering all the interview questions, the 14-year-old takes over the conversation. Leo wants to discuss the essential purpose of school curricula, before criticising that "Nobody teaches us how to do a tax return or how to put a bicycle chain back on." He recently had to help out a classmate with her bike, which – in his opinion – is one of the easiest things in the world to do.

Leo is sitting in the quiet room in his school's media centre. He is surrounded by all the books one would expect in a school library: German books, dictionaries, atlases, books on sociology and politics, young adult novels in English. He sees a lack of the "basic things that really help you later in life. That you know a little bit about the law and about what rights you have, and what the legal options are if something goes wrong." He thinks for a minute and then adds, "In our globalised world, it's important to know how the economy works." He'd also like to learn more about computer programming, "so that you theoretically know how one robot is able to raise up a car and how the other robot is able to paint it." Leo could take computer science as an elective, but he wants more than that.

A study asked Germans aged 15 to 24 which content-related knowledge, social skills and competencies they thought should be taught at school, and which of them actually are.[2] In their answers, they make plain that what is missing are so-called life hacks: 63 percent think schools should teach students how to correctly and safely engage with social networks, protect personal data and use apps; only 18 percent have actually learned how. There is a similarly large gap when it comes to financial issues: 69 percent think they should be addressed in school, but only 12 percent say they have been. As many as 61 percent of young people consider knowledge about nature, the environment and climate protection important, but only 41 percent feel they have sufficiently discussed the issues in class. There is also a large discrepancy in teaching social behaviour; this study did not consider the question of classes on the law, as Leo calls for, but there would most likely be a large disparity here, as well.

However, schools score well when it comes to their ability to train students in speaking in front of others or giving presentations. Students also feel relatively well-prepared when using common computer programmes such as Word and PowerPoint, or in discussing political issues. Young people are reasonably satisfied with the way their school teaches them to support and stand up for others, and to express themselves and get their ideas across. Generation Z does not fundamentally criticise their schools wholesale, if only because they appreciate the personal commitment of their teachers. They do, however, want to be better prepared for life and trained for active participation in their communities.

It is Wednesday, seventh period. In history class, Jana and Merle turn on the projector. They begin a presentation that will last just under an hour. Topic: What foundations did ancient Greek democracy lay for the post-war Basic Law of the Federal Republic of Germany? The two twelfth-graders begin with a clip from a documentary produced by one of Germany's public broadcasters on the origins of the Basic Law. Following a powerful musical intro and the cliff-hanger question of whether the fathers and mothers of the Basic Law could bring themselves to abolish the death penalty, Merle and Jana rewind more than 2,500 years back to antiquity.

During their presentation, Jana and Merle switch between presentation mode, discussions with their classmates and tables they have compiled with the most important differences and similarities between the ancient Greek and German constitutions. They use PowerPoint and the smartboard with confidence. At the end, their fellow students applaud. In the feedback round, Christoph Köhn, their history teacher, puts the question of democracy aside for the time being, calling instead for praise and suggestions for the presentation itself. In addition to the lesson plan for each subject, the Sophie Scholl school has also developed a methods curriculum that establishes which methodology is taught in which subject in which grade. It is precisely this way of interweaving subject matter learning and skills training that young people have come to expect of their teachers. Because subject knowledge is not enough to get ahead in the knowledge economy anymore, the ability to translate that knowledge into different contexts and apply it across various scenarios is.

Learning about the climate crisis

Young people would love to systematically learn about climate change and sustainable development. But in Germany, the climate crisis is unlikely to become an independent school subject in the foreseeable future. The Ministries of Education of the 16 federal states have thus far fought off any attempt to change or expand the existing canon of class subjects, especially since it would also mean radically transforming the foundation of teacher education in the country. In Germany, teachers receive specific training in two academic subjects as part of their teaching degrees and, subsequently, are only certified to teach those two subjects.[3]

What the ministries have instead called for is cross-subject teaching plans. For issues like the environment and climate, this idea actually makes sense: In physics class, students learn about the greenhouse effect; in geography class, they learn about its consequences. In addition, biology lessons highlight the effects on flora and fauna, while a social science teacher can guide students through the possibilities for a climate-neutral restructuring of society and of political decision-making processes. For a crisis that demands answers in almost all areas of life, this is an appropriate approach, in particular since it requires competence in very different subjects.

Although the climate crisis is at the forefront of Generation Z's collective attention, only a few schools systematically deal with the issue of environmental change and its long-term consequences. Others make a token gesture just before the major school holidays by squeezing in a project week that includes a couple of speakers from Greenpeace and a smattering of interesting video clips from the internet. If there is enough time, there is the option to discuss the UN Framework Convention on Climate Change or to determine the ecological footprint of each individual student. For Generation Z, such disappointing showings are not how they imagine a school that meets the challenges of the day.

Social behaviour

When Tom goes out on the playground at Rosenhöhe Secondary School, he puts on a white high-visibility vest with the school logo emblazoned on his chest – a stylised rose blossom with colourful figures instead of leaves. During the break, his gaze roams over the schoolyard in search of conflicts. "When there's trouble, you can go over, separate the kids and if necessary, call over a teacher." Tom is a breaktime scout (or facilitator) at his school. Sometimes, when a sixth grader is afraid of an older student, he accompanies them back to classroom after the break in order to reassure them.

What once might have been considered uncool is now hip; teachers have noticed that for Generation Z, it is all about being there for each other. Sixty percent would like to learn how to better advocate and be there for others, but only 34 percent say that their school has taught them such skills. In addition, they would like to be taught appropriate social behaviour and etiquette (54 percent of those surveyed; only 17 percent have been taught social skills at school).[4]

Although they are often notably fond of their parents, Generation Z acknowledges that their immediate family is unable to fully prepare them for every aspect of modern life – which is why they want schools to take on more of those responsibilities previously assigned to their parents, with teachers expected to be responsive to every concern and need. The formerly clear division between school and home life, wherein school imparts knowledge while the family nurtures, shapes personalities and sets expectations in terms of culture, values and manners, has begun to melt away as modern life has become more complicated.

Today's adolescents feel they have to make far more complex decisions than their parents and grandparents ever did. The opportunities for individual self-expression have increased exponentially, as have the multitude of degrees to choose from, the nearly unlimited options for leisure time and media use, and the opportunities to express personal values that are much less determined by family background than in the past. While Generation Z now has access to an infinite number of ways to live their lives according to their individual goals and needs, nothing is set in stone – raising the risks of failure for many of these young people.

In response to these changing dynamics, Generation Z wants schools, the educational institution par excellence, to teach them the skills they need to make full use of the opportunities that lie ahead of them, adding to the already long to-do list confronting schools in the twenty-first century.

Generation Z is actively requesting binding rules with which to organise their school communities; ideally, they are drafted by students and teachers together, with parents consulted whenever possible. These kinds of social contracts can help deal with violence and aggressive behaviour at school. Developing them takes time and effort, but it is very much worth it. Schools with binding agreements have a much higher success rate at preventing violence than those without.

There are 13 other break scouts at Tom's school. They usually wander the schoolyard in twos or threes to solve conflicts or call on a teacher. "We've also talked about how we can spot trouble better and faster" – yet another way school can teach social behaviour.

Health education in schools

Modern life puts major demands on students' ability to perform. In a society where individuality and autonomy are prized above all else, self-directed and self-determined action has become the key to success. Knowledge of the body and healthy living has thus become a much more important resource for today's young people. Only those who have the opportunities to acquire the necessary health literacy can then foster the "resilience" needed today. Health literacy ensures personal well-being and stabilises physical and mental health – it is the elixir of life in modern societies.[5] In the age of the coronavirus pandemic, public awareness of this has never been greater.

Current studies show that adolescents and young adults are insufficiently literate in matters of health, which they blame on their schools. An overwhelming majority (80 percent) of young adults in Germany are interested in the introduction of health as a subject at school. Only 25 percent have received health education beyond sex ed. at school – mostly on nutrition, dental care, common diseases, prevention or the structure of the healthcare system.

There is thus much to be said for including health literacy in the curriculum of primary and secondary schools, universities, youth education and vocational training institutions. The coronavirus crisis has also spurred a growing number of teachers to speak out in favour of making health education a standard part of the curriculum.

Economics class

Back in the green classroom at Sophie Scholl Secondary School. The school shop now sells pesto, bread and honey fresh from the school garden, along with its long-time bestseller: school supplies. Students have come up with their own ideas, such as fanny packs and USB sticks bearing the school logo. "There used to be a sweatshirt, I have it here," says Juliane Westphal, the head teacher, as she pulls out one with the school logo and a portrait of Sophie Scholl, a student and anti-Nazi activist who was executed in 1943. "On the back is a statement by Sophie Scholl chosen by the students."

The school also plans to introduce economics as a subject in the coming years. According to Westphal, the focus will be on the basic principles of economic activity, such as the difference between revenue and profit and the rules of elementary accounting, which could then be put into practice in the green classroom. In addition, more student companies affiliated with the urban gardening project are to be established.

The young generation actively calls for this kind of lesson planning. Fifty-two percent of young people think that schools should teach economics, but only 32 percent believe that the subject is sufficiently taught.[6] Without these classes, schools deprive their students of knowledge about a key area of social and political life. Every student is confronted in their daily lives with situations that require economic knowledge – from handling pocket money or opening a bank account to making consumer decisions. The fair allocation of scarce resources, questions of sustainability and efficient production – these are all issues that schools should discuss so that students can make competent decisions and act appropriately.

Expert studies have shown that young people aged 17 to 27 deal extensively with financial and economic issues. A surprising number of them are on the look-out for ways to set aside money and to save for later in life, including retirement.[7] A meaningful, practical introduction to economic thinking and acting in everyday life requires the inclusion of economics in the curriculum, if only to lay the groundwork for an understanding of economic issues and an openness to independence and economic risk.

The euro crisis, trade wars, the taxation of the big tech corporations – many of the major political flashpoints today revolve around economic issues. Here too, schools are needed to help turn young people into responsible citizens. By integrating economics, financial and retirement planning into the lesson plan and into daily school life, schools would be able to respond to the daily challenges facing the younger generation. The complexity, differentiations and dynamics of economic life require the systematic acquisition of skills that enable young people to understand, assess and shape their society in a competent, critical and responsible manner.

These arguments are beginning to bear fruit, especially as young people are not alone in their criticism. As social and economic associations and certain political parties have begun to advocate for its inclusion, Baden-Württemberg and North Rhine-Westphalia, two of Germany's larger federal states, have bowed to pressure and will introduce economics as a school subject – which will also require the inclusion of economics as one of the possible disciplines chosen as part of a teaching degree.

School strikes as leverage

The introduction of economics as a new subject brings schools a step closer to the social reality of today's young people and was only achieved through enormous pressure exercised upon both state governments in Baden-Württemberg and North Rhine-Westphalia – including by the younger generation.

In its own way, the Fridays for Future movement has also attempted to put various governments and political parties under pressure. Before schools began to close in response to the coronavirus pandemic, the movement used school strikes as a new form of protest. Many German students followed Greta Thunberg's call and skipped school on Fridays to demonstrate for changes to national and international environmental policy.

Since school is compulsory in Germany (and home-schooling is illegal under most circumstances), these strikes represented an unauthorised absence from school, which violates federal state law and is punishable by fine or – if repeated – even prison or the withdrawal of custody for the legal guardian. Students of legal age can be fined or forced to perform community service.

Greta Thunberg and Fridays for Future have provided a radical justification for the flouting of this regulation: It is more important to save the world than to obey the law and attend school. The magnitude and immediacy of the existential problem of climate change makes school strikes more than legitimate. "And why should I be studying for a future that soon will be no more, when no one is doing anything whatsoever to save that future?" Thunberg has asked. "And what is the point of learning facts within the school system when the most important facts given by the finest science of that same school system clearly mean nothing to our politicians and our society?"[8]

Although indirect, Thunberg's sharp critique of school as an institution builds upon the notion that the knowledge and skills her generation are taught in the classroom do not consider the epochal challenges of the future. That failure justifies the school strikes: The fight against the climate crisis is more important than good grades.

The strikes triggered much criticism in Germany and attracted a great deal of public attention. After a few weeks, however, students were able to shift the conversation away from their breaking of the rules to the motivation for doing so – putting the climate crisis at the centre of the public discussion. Many parents sympathised with their children's struggle, as did a large majority of their teachers. Contrary to instructions issued by authorities, they convinced school administrators to respond flexibly to "absences from school." Some schools considered a note from parents enough to keep their children's absenteeism from appearing on report cards, despite technically being required by law to administer some form of punishment. School administrators and teaching staff were thus able to voice their support for their students by accepting that the strikes did not represent quotidian acts of truancy but were an expression of their deeply held political convictions.

This shift in the popular conversation around Fridays for Future helped the movement achieve two goals at once: Following Greta Thunberg's example in Stockholm, it managed to push the climate issue to the forefront of the political debate, forcing politicians to act (or at a minimum address the issue). This demonstrates the strategic finesse of this young movement. It also succeeded in initiating a debate on the creation of meaningful course contents and suitable forms of knowledge and skills transfer in schools.

Notes

1 Köcher et al. 2019, p. 53.
2 Köcher et al. 2019, p. 51.
3 KMK 2015.
4 Köcher et al. 2019, p. 53.
5 Hurrelmann and Richter 2020.
6 Köcher et al. 2019, p. 52.
7 Hurrelmann et al. 2019, p. 29.
8 Thunberg 2019, p. 25.

Chapter 9

Who falls through the cracks?
The experience of disadvantaged youth

A wide performance gap

"With the shrill squeal of the brakes still in his ears, Redluff watched the face of the driver twist in anger," Juliane Westphal reads aloud. "He staggers two steps back onto the sidewalk." Twenty-seven seventh-grade students listen to their teacher read from Herbert Malecha's short story, "Die Probe" (The Test), a 1954 classic that is still regularly taught in German schools, in a sunny classroom at Sophie Scholl Secondary School. Most of them are hanging on her every word. Only in the back rows can a rustling be heard. Even digital natives still pass notes the old-fashioned way: on paper under their desks. After a few minutes, Westphal stops reading. "What just happened here?" she asks the class.

Based on Malecha's narrative, the class is supposed to develop an understanding of a literary text's narrative perspective. For homework, they will retell the story of Redluff, an apprehensive criminal who dares to go out on the streets for the first time with a forged passport and is promptly stopped by the police, from the perspective of the other protagonists. But first, Westphal wants to make sure that everyone in the class has understood the story's plot.

A few doors further down the hall, Christoph Köhn and his eighth-grade students are working on a different text. While one student fetches his textbook from his locker at the back of the classroom, Köhn asks a student in the second row to start reading aloud. The 14-year-old reads the English text fluently, only stumbling a bit on the pronunciation of "alarming-ly." The non-fiction text discusses stop and frisk, the practice made (in)famous by the New York City police, who stop people arbitrarily and search them for drugs or illegal weapons. Ninety percent of those stopped are Black.

At the end, Köhn asks a few comprehension questions based on the text. Despite the fact that the text is in a foreign language, his questions are more detailed than Westphal's. The class summarises the material and discusses the author's perspective towards stop and frisk. Köhn then uses the text to introduce the present perfect progressive, by letting his students explore the new tense themselves: "I would like you to figure out what the rules are."

Closely supervised hands-on teaching in one class, independent learning in the other – at this secondary school in Berlin, the wide range of contemporary teaching and learning styles is on display up and down the corridor. In Köhn's class, the students are working towards a joint French baccalauréat and German Abitur in Westphal's class, on the other hand, the students are striving for a secondary school-leaving certificate.

The division between these two classes runs right through Generation Z. On the one hand, there are students like Nele and Karl. Nele knows that she wants to study medicine; Karl would first like to focus on acing his school-leaving examinations. He can see himself studying many different things, including medicine (his parents are doctors). Both students have signed up for the Junior Engineering Academy as an elective at their school. There, students conduct independent research, in cooperation with the local technical college. Nele and Karl have also started learning a third foreign language. In a class in which hoodies are part of the basic attire, Karl wears a light beige knit sweater. Sometimes it bothers him that he spends so much time every day at school, he says. "But actually, I'm completely satisfied right now."

Both belong to the approximately 40 percent of Gen Zers who are considered strong performers, the Gretas, so to speak. Most of them come from affluent families, enjoy school, possess the ability to reflect on their skills and development, and are self-disciplined. They are not only politically involved but also show initiative in class and school life.

Then there are students like Jolina or Emil. Jolina is still thinking about whether she would like to start an apprenticeship or go to university. Emil wants to enter the fashion industry. The right sleeve of his black hoodie is white; the left sleeve is ochre. The 14-year-old sewed it together himself from three old sweatshirts. "Maths doesn't do much for me," Emil admits frankly. "But I know I need it for my Abitur." But paying attention in religion class is really difficult for him. Jolina also wants to get her Abitur – and faces similar challenges. "A lot of things are really difficult for me," she says. "Like maths." Still, school is important to her "because it determines the future." Jolina and Emil belong to Gen Z's second 40 percent – the average performers. They will make their way, albeit with greater difficulty. These too will both likely obtain their Abitur, although most in this group leave school after ten years with a secondary school-leaving certificate that does not make them automatically eligible for university.

Finally, there are students like Joy and Tom. Tom has been stopped from attending his second advanced course because of poor performance. As a result, he cannot take the three higher-level subjects he needs to graduate with a secondary school-leaving certificate at the end of the year. He is currently applying for positions as a retail apprentice. Joy would like to be a flight attendant, but knows that she needs the secondary school-leaving certificate before she can apply to attend flight attendant training. In the end, both of them will only be able to complete the basic degree, available after nine years, at the end of the term.

The weakest group, those 20 percent with the most unfavourable starting conditions, is finding it increasingly difficult to make its way after leaving school. Like Joy and Tom, they are lucky to finish school with a basic qualification. But even before the coronavirus slump, during an economic upswing and a shortage of skilled workers, it was not easy for this group to find an apprenticeship or entry-level position. In the looming post-coronavirus economic downturn, they are by far the most vulnerable group.

The Gretas among the Generation Zers – the highly-motivated students who will in all likelihood attend university afterwards – also set the tone at school. Almost half of Generation Z attends more academically oriented (versus vocationally oriented) Gymnasium today,[1] where girls are especially successful; 53 percent attend such schools, compared with only 42 percent of boys.

Gymnasium attendance leads directly to the Abitur, and this is what Gen Z is all about. Even before the coronavirus pandemic, the Abitur was the trump card. In Germany, it is not only the most prestigious school-leaving certificate, but also the one that guarantees the legal right to study at a university. When asked which school-leaving certificate they would like to obtain, 69 percent of adolescents indicated that their goal is the Abitur – despite the fact that most academically oriented secondary schools continue to be very conventional and teach the traditional subjects in a teacher-centred mode.[2] In fact, well over 50 percent of young people today leave school with the Abitur, a trend that continues to increase. The economic collapse caused by the coronavirus pandemic will likely also further encourage this trend, just as every other crisis before it has. The Abitur has thus become the gold standard of German education. Parents want their children to graduate because it gives them the most options for the future: vocational training, university studies, a combination of the two or a dual university education.

The teacher-student flat

"This is our living room," says Stefanie Grigo,[3] the sweep of her arm indicating a loft-like area. The space must have once been a classroom, but, now, the school corridor widens into an open space. Pop art portraits of ninth grade students hang on the wall and a collection of hipster lemonade beverage crates serve as stools around a long, low table. Floor-to-ceiling windows provide a view of the staff room.

Grigo calls the room a "teacher-student flat." The setting would be more reminiscent of a start-up office, if not for the noise from the playground coming through the large windows. Grigo used to teach German and home economics at a Hauptschule – a type of school that is now being phased out that was geared towards completion of the basic school-leaving qualification as a prerequisite for a low-skill vocational apprenticeship. Today, she teaches at Rosenhöhe Secondary School in Bielefeld.

For decades, school policy in Germany has involved debate over the merits and disadvantages of its three-tiered educational system. After only four years of primary school, students are channelled into a pre-university track (Gymnasium), an intermediate track that qualifies students for vocational training (Realschule) and a basic track that meets the compulsory school attendance requirement and qualifies students for low-skill apprenticeships (Hauptschule) – according to their level of achievement at the time.

Generation Z is the first generation for whom this selection no longer applies. In Germany, educational issues are under the purview of the federal states, and many of them have decided to combine Hauptschule and Realschule into comprehensive schools that offer several types of school-leaving certificates. Many of them now also include the option of completing the Abitur after an additional two or three years of schooling. The three-tiered school system is slowly being replaced by a two-tiered system.

Nonetheless, Gymnasium remains highly attractive. Very few high achievers are inclined to attend other types of secondary school, and as a result, comprehensive schools lack the diversity their pedagogical strategy is ostensibly aiming for. The job of teachers at such schools has become increasingly difficult in recent years.

Rosenhöhe Secondary School in Bielefeld is witness to this shift. The school has over 1,100 students, a good 900 from fifth to tenth grade. Rosenhöhe's approach is directed at a multicultural student body with a heterogeneous social structure. The proportion of those who lack basic German language skills is relatively large. The school has just become a "Talent School," a programme sponsored by the state government that provides additional support for so-called "high risk" schools. For Rosenhöhe, this means more teachers, more professional development for those teachers and a focus on mathematics, the natural sciences and technology.

Teachers actively emphasise collaborative learning, says André Koch,[4] an English teacher, which is reflected in the room's set-up. The door to the space remains open during class time. "Group work can be done outside, so it's a little quieter for the rest of the students," he explains. "Theoretically, you can do a bunch of different things: a listening task in here and, outside, a quiet task such as station learning."

In theory, this type of collaborative learning works well for a class of 27 students. "The problem we have here is that the whole of the class is relatively weak," says Koch. Most of the better-performing students from the elementary schools in the neighbourhood chose the closest Gymnasium instead. In Koch's class, only two out of 27 students had the primary school grades to do so. Without stronger students who can help their classmates to understand the text or answer questions during group work, Koch says, there is a lack of support for the weaker ones. Establishing mixed performance learning groups has thus become increasingly difficult for teachers like Grigo and Koch. The result is that low-performing students are often left on their own.

Not only in Bielefeld, but all over Germany, educational inequality has not diminished in the last 15 years; on the contrary, studies show that the gap has even increased in some areas, such as reading comprehension among 15-year-olds. While one segment of Germany's young people is particularly competent in reading and performs in the top tier in international comparisons, there are also those at the lower end that lag behind those in other countries. The gap between the two groups is greater in Germany than in any other participating OECD country. And the gap, when compared to previous OECD-PISA studies, has continued to grow.[5] This is mainly due to the long-standing tradition in the German educational system of placing children onto particular educational tracks with far-reaching consequences after only four years of elementary school.

The educationally disadvantaged are only too aware of this situation. When asked about his intentions in terms of a school-leaving certification, Tom, one of the tenth-grade students at Rosenhöhe Secondary School, answers with a question of his own: "What we are aiming for or what we would like most?" After being thrown out of the advanced course needed for a secondary school-leaving certificate "without a peep from the teachers," he is set to graduate with only a basic qualification certificate at the end of the school year and he intends to leave it that way. "But otherwise, I'd want get my Abitur. Why not have the best?" The Abitur helps even when applying for apprenticeships that formally only require a basic qualification, he explains.

And he is right. The basic qualification after nine years of schooling no longer suffices to apply for an apprenticeship. In an increasing number of professions, graduates with this qualification have very poor chances as soon as a possible competitor with a secondary school qualification or Abitur comes into play. Many apprenticeships are advertised from the outset as only for graduates with at least an intermediate, comprehensive school certificate. If a company can recruit an apprentice with an Abitur, other applicants no longer stand a chance.

Tom's classmate, Cihan, is 15 years old and determined to get his Abitur after obtaining his secondary school certificate (an option if his grades are good enough), "because it just opens up more doors for me." It also gives him more time to consider a career path. This trend towards Abitur leaves little room for late bloomers or young people with other skill sets, and many academically weak students are discouraged by the effects of credential creep (where, over time, the same job requires ever greater qualifications despite the job itself remaining the same). While graduates with good school-leaving certificates are spoilt by a multitude of choices and can carefully decide on a career path most suitable to them, opportunities for weaker students have become much more limited. The approximately seven percent of every cohort nationwide that does not complete even the basic qualification stand almost no chance of finding an apprenticeship today.

Tom completed one of his mandatory school internships at a video production company in Bielefeld, but has not included them on his list of possible employers. "It's out of my league," he says. "You need an Abitur for that."

Social background is decisive

When André Koch, the teacher at Rosenhöhe School in Bielefeld, begins the lesson about hyperinflation during the Weimar Republic, he shows students photos of children playing with money. "Then I ask, 'What do you see?' The questions start immediately: 'Why are they playing with money? Isn't it worth anything? What's up with the money?'" Once the class is hooked, he explains how inflation works with the help of a game. "Let's assume that these sweets represent everything that can be bought and sold in our country; there's nothing else. And now you each get money." Based on the amount of candy, it is easy to see how much it would cost. Then Koch doubles the amount of money. "Then it also becomes clear, that if the money supply doubles, every piece of candy must be twice as expensive. And then they realise that increasing the money supply makes the money worth less, and that's inflation." And suddenly, the cause of the 1923 hyperinflation becomes clear.

Most of the students in his class have a family history of migration, 50 percent struggle with the German language – especially when it comes to technical terms. To accommodate them, the school has instituted language-sensitive classes. "Thirty percent definitely still make grammatical errors in tenth grade," says Koch. Reading skills are also not fully developed.

Therefore, as in the lesson on hyperinflation, he focuses on learning via pictures or games, so that all students can actively participate. Learning through texts can always come later. In the meantime, "I really have to encourage them to read," including through collaborative reading, where students read a text together and then talk about it. "The important thing is that when they read with a partner, they take the trouble to understand the text and don't say, 'I can read it, but I can't make sense of it.'"

In Germany, a child's school-leaving certificate is even more closely related to the educational level attained by its parents than in other countries.[6] As a reaction to interventions by the Nazis in family life, the Basic Law of the Federal Republic of Germany grants parents the primary role in the education of their children. Public educational institutions are deliberately assigned a secondary role. For this reason, all-day schools are only slowly becoming the norm. Teachers do not dare to get involved beyond offering professional suggestions, which leaves adolescents from less academically focused parental homes with little support from school.

"If I tell my mother I don't want to do my homework and I'll do it tomorrow, she says, 'Then don't do it,'" says Tom. "She says I'm not going to school for her, I'm going to school for me."

"Parents are really very insecure these days about how to raise their children," observes Stefanie Grigo, Tom's teacher. She feels young people need more guidance. "They need someone who can really give them direction: 'This is how it's done, these are the steps, now let's sit down together and do it.'" Grigo knows that parents play a huge role in child development – more so today than in the past. "Family systems have, of course, radically changed. Women are employed. In the past, they took over much more control and support than they do and can do today." There are many working single mothers among the parents in her class. "It's hard for them to balance everything."

Germany still has a long way to go here. Even 20 years ago, schools offering lunch to their pupils were virtually non-existent. In most cases, class ended at 1 p.m. Although this has dramatically changed in recent years, even today, only 13 percent of families have two full-time working parents; in the rest it is predominantly the father who holds a full-time position. The number of full-time employed women has been increasing constantly in recent years. Still, single mothers in particular lack the support structures needed.

This is especially true when a household's economic situation is teetering on the edge: Three million children nationwide live in relatively poor families, with a household income that is less than 60 percent of the national average. Poverty thus directly affects every fifth child. In particular, children of single parents are at risk of living in poverty, with a large proportion of such families receiving basic social benefits which barely help make ends meet.

Children from these families are not only economically deprived – they also suffer from very low educational attainment. Most of them would like to obtain a much higher school-leaving certificate than their own parents, but lack the necessary competencies. Students with a family history of migration are no different from other families that share a similarly low socioeconomic status. Rather, the parents' level of education determines childrens' success at school. Ethnic or religious factors have little impact.[7]

This is not unique to Germany. In *The Spirit Level*, authors Richard Wilkinson and Kate Pickett quote a study showing that three-year-olds from disadvantaged backgrounds were already lagging up to one year behind their more privileged peers.[8] The UK government's commission on social mobility found in 2019 that by age 11 "less than half (46 per cent) of pupils entitled to free school meals reach the standards expected for reading, writing and mathematics, compared to 68 per cent of all other pupils."[9]

Overall, the proportion of children from all types of families living in relative poverty has risen steadily both in the UK and in Germany over the past decade. Parents are insecure about their financial situations and are so busy organising daily life that they lack the time and energy to adequately prepare their children for school. This often has health-related consequences: impaired self-esteem, a disturbed relationship to their bodies and to self-care. In Berlin-Schöneberg, Juliane Westphal, the head teacher, has also witnessed an increase in problems faced by the children: "One trend is that a lot of children come with a lot of baggage: broken families, helpless parents, personal misfortune, the list goes on."

When she employs tablets to teach her seventh grade students in the remedial German class, she notices how motivated the students are, despite everything. "They're eager. They don't break things and they don't throw the tablets out the window, which they could just as well do." In truth, they want attention. "They want someone to come and tell them, 'Look, this is how it's done.'"

Parents with less formal education often find it difficult to actively support their children's education. Teachers at comprehensive secondary schools are confronted with this issue every day. "I have the feeling that at an academically oriented Gymnasium, learning happens more at home than at school," says André Koch from Rosenhöhe Secondary School in Bielefeld. "Because educational achievement depends on whether the students learn at home what they should be learning in class."

His school wants to do things differently. "We try to take the students out of their homes," says Koch. "We also try to compensate for it by giving them room to learn." The students have two hours per week of study time at school, during which they do their homework and receive the help their parents might be unable to give them. Although it is not enough in Koch's opinion, it is much more than at an average secondary school, where the deal is usually, "Here's your homework, now go home."

"At my old school, it was sink or swim. I had to figure everything out for myself. Here, everything's explained to me," says Cihan, who transferred from an academically oriented Gymnasium to Rosenhöhe Secondary School. "I didn't feel comfortable there anymore because of the teachers," says the 15-year-old. "I got lower grades, which I didn't like." When he saw no other way out, he transferred to the comprehensive secondary school.

Lower-performing students like Cihan often blame teachers for their less-than-stellar grades. They do not have the ability to self-assess their strengths and weaknesses or only have a low degree of self-discipline. "Among the supposedly weaker students, there are some who do an awful lot," observes André Koch, who teaches English as well as social studies. "They try hard but sometimes take the wrong approach. They work a lot, but they're not focused." Some highlight texts from top to bottom, others write far too much in the margins. "This is an incredible achievement, but it doesn't help them understand the text and break down the content." As a result, weaker students often feel overwhelmed. "The other thing is that many say, 'If I try hard and still don't succeed, then I won't try anymore.'"

It's a guy thing

"I take school more seriously now than I did before," Cihan says dutifully after explaining his transfer between schools. At this, his classmate, Tom, bursts out laughing: "No way!" "Sooner or later you have to take it seriously," Cihan insists. "At some point, it clicks and you say, yeah, okay, now I gotta do something."

"It still hasn't clicked for him yet," interjects Tom, still laughing. He does not mean to be insulting; he counts himself among those who are still waiting for it to 'click.' Cihan thinks for a moment, and then continues. Laziness is the biggest problem. "You know it's important, but once you're lying on the sofa, you don't want to get up."

Young men from educationally disadvantaged backgrounds, such as Tom and Cihan, are most affected by educational poverty. They have the most difficulty in finding their way in our modern knowledge society; in comparison, young women in particular have benefited from expanded educational opportunities. Whereas in the 1960s they still belonged to a heavily disadvantaged group, today they make up the majority in pre-university secondary schools. They are more likely to receive their Abitur and more likely to be admitted to competitive university programmes with selective admission.[10] What the statistics for Germany and other European countries show on the macro level, Cihan and Tom represent on the micro level: When they copy homework from a classmate, they prefer a "high-performing girl," as Tom puts it. "You just know that the girls have worked harder. They probably have reread the texts. Guys say to themselves, 'I'll just write something down, maybe it'll be right.'" "If I copy from guys, I may as well just copy from Wikipedia," says Cihan with a laugh. Then he tries to save the honour of his male brethren: "If a guy likes a subject, I think he does better than the girls," he explains. "But if a guy doesn't like a subject, you can do what you want…he'll always find an excuse."

Stefanie Grigo has also observed that girls are, on average, much more organised than boys. "It is very difficult, especially for boys, to write down and mentally file away what they've learned in class," she says. Tom had planned to work through his weekly maths assignment the night before. "Then I thought: 'Nope, I'll just tell my teacher tomorrow that I forgot and do it tomorrow.'" Today is his last chance; if he does not finish it, he will have to stay after school. The pressure helps, Tom says. "I've never been to detention." "Unfortunately, not everybody possesses good old discipline," Grigo says. "You have to go over everything with them in very small steps, in terms of what they need to do to reach their goal." This mainly holds for the boys. In contrast, girls and young women are more adept at practising the virtue of self-discipline and self-organisation. Grigo believes that this may be because girls tend to take on more tasks within the family. They have learned to adapt to the complex demands of a social system.

"Girls want things to work. They get good feedback when they're social." And they are often more ambitious and receive more support at school. One of the reasons why many young men find the social aspect of school so difficult is that they lack male role models in everyday life.[11] Below university level, there are more female teachers in all educational institutions, but the gender imbalance is especially prevalent in kindergartens, primary and secondary schools.

Young men also have greater difficulty in coping with how the role of masculinity in society is changing. At school, for example, they still worry about being considered wimpy or nerdy. Many awkwardly escape into primitive macho patterns of masculinity and act like cowboys, which is unlikely to be conducive to their educational performance.[12] This recourse to traditional gender roles points to the severe strain caused by social change and often leads to a number of negative consequences – from "heroic" resistance to school and a tendency towards "male" risk behaviour in leisure activities to an increased propensity for violence and a heightened inclination to committing crime. This behaviour is ultimately a reaction to the lack – or perceived lack – of opportunities and access to a stable and secure future.

Being a status fatalist

In recent years, studies have noted an increasing uncertainty and diminished optimism about the future, particularly among adolescents at poorly performing schools. This affects boys in particularly, many of whom have lost access to many of the traditional employment opportunities available to previous generations, as deindustrialisation has shifted the labour market away from labour-intensive industrial work. These young men feel increasingly resigned, which in turn has a negative impact on their motivation at school. Many fear that the economic and labour market crisis triggered by the coronavirus pandemic will further intensify this development.

Boys who are unsuccessful at school seek approval and recognition elsewhere, and often find it in the peer group. "For me, when I say I'm going home to study, my friends write: 'Let's meet up online,'" explains Cihan. "Then you say, 'Okay, today I'll go online and then study tomorrow.' The next day you don't want to. And it's like this over and over, until one day at school it's like, shit…there's a test in class today!"

Young men need support not only in terms of their performance but also in terms of social skills – in learning and practising how to engage with others, including preventing violence and dealing with conflict. A central task is to convey to young men that life in a community, in which they have to accept certain principles and guidelines, can be fun and enjoyable. This includes developing a sensitivity for the interests of others, as well an ability to perceive everyday aggression and admit to being affected by violence.

Tom and Cihan have managed to escape these patterns. Tom regularly patrols the playground as a break facilitator, and in this way, does his part to help prevent violence and build community at school. He also likes to help people, which is one of the reasons why he is applying for apprenticeships in retail. At the absolute latest, when he is grown up and has a job he does not like, says Cihan, he will understand why school is important. "Then you regret that you messed up at school or didn't pay any attention to begin with," he adds with a laugh.

Nearly 20 percent of young adults agree with the statement: "It is true that some are on top and others are at the bottom, and based on current circumstances are unable to reach the top no matter how hard they try." Among respondents from families with a very low social and financial status, 31 percent agree with this fatalistic position.[13] A "status fatalist" is someone who believes that they are unable to improve their economic situation through their own efforts. These young people cannot avoid the feeling that they are marginalised. No matter what they do, they feel like they have no leverage to improve their situation. International comparative studies conducted by the OECD confirm how difficult it is to free oneself from a position at the margins of society.[14]

Germany has a welfare system which prefers supporting those who already have a position in society, such as adults in the work force. What is left by the wayside, in comparison to other countries, is a strategy to strengthen and support society at large by means of greater investments in the education system and youth – those who have yet to achieve something.

Germany only invests six percent of its gross national product in education. In comparison, most OECD countries, and especially the Scandinavian countries, invest approximately ten percent. Ten percent is also the proportion of the budget that all federal state education ministers and the chancellor agreed to spend as part of an education pact for Germany signed several years ago. But little has happened since then, which is why a much too large segment of Generation Z is getting a raw deal, even in a job market that has (until recently) been booming.

Notes

1 Leven et al. 2019b, p. 166.
2 Leven et al. 2019b, p. 167.
3 Name changed.

4 Name changed.
5 OECD 2018, p. 55.
6 OECD 2018, p. 62.
7 Hurrelmann and Bauer 2018, p. 135.
8 Wilkinson and Pickett 2011, p. 110
9 Social Mobility Commission 2019, p. 37
10 Hurrelmann and Quenzel 2012.
11 Kiselica et al. 2016.
12 Quenzel and Hurrelmann 2013.
13 Köcher et al. 2019, p. 26.
14 OECD 2018, p. 64.

Chapter 10

Jobs in transition
Navigating a shifting labour market

Contradictions within the labour market

"There was a question just now on why these blood vessels are so dark," says Maciej Mularczyk in English. "These are the veins." With two casual flicks of his finger, the lecturer exposes the major veins in the upper arm during an anatomy lesson for first-year students at the Pomeranian Medical University in Szczecin, Poland. A dozen students listen attentively; they are part of a growing number of young Germans whose path to medical school takes them to Eastern Europe. In Szczecin, almost half of the medical students in the two English-language programmes come from Germany. Their degrees are recognised throughout the EU.

The students wear white coats but the corpse in front of them exists only in the virtual world: Mularczyk is using a simulated dissection table controlled by touchscreen; without hesitating, he turns it over to one of the students. Otto intrepidly cuts into the torso on the screen and, layer by layer, dissects the virtual arm. More veins appear under the muscle until he hits the bone.

Otto graduated from pre-university secondary school with a 2.1 grade point average (approximately an upper second class degree or a B+ GPA), a solid degree but not good enough to be admitted to a medical school in Germany, which has become extremely selective in recent years, requiring an eye-popping 1.1 average due to a strict limit on the number of new admissions. "No one here could get in with their grade point average," says Otto. "But we all really wanted to go to medical school." Studying in Poland, however, is no easier than in Germany or anywhere else, says Otto. "We're all ambitious, sometimes we're up until three in the morning, studying the body and analysing how it's built."

The next generation of doctors will be able to choose their own path in the profession, with doctors desperately needed in several sub-specialities and geographical regions. University in Germany is tuition-free and financed by taxpayer money, but the number of available spots in sought-after disciplines such as medicine is restricted through the so-called 'numerus clausus' (NC) which sets a maximum number of admissions for the whole country. This leads many secondary school graduates to believe that the NC is an artificial shortage caused by specific political policies. As a result, more and more are turning to universities in other European countries, which are happy to accept them in exchange for what are usually high tuition fees. Altogether, approximately 40 percent of all university programmes are restricted by an NC; only those students with an excellent grade point average are admitted immediately to medicine, psychology, pharmacy and law. This is one of the many contradictions on the labour market that awaits highly qualified Generation Zers. They typically graduate with an Abitur, and still have to worry about snagging a spot in their programme of choice, despite a university system that is ostensibly open to anyone with that qualification. Those with mediocre grades can wait years for admission, gaining their spot through a complicated system of "waiting semesters" during which they are not enrolled in a university programme.

The younger generation is thus faced with a labour and educational market that is becoming increasingly difficult to navigate, despite the fact that their participation is urgently needed.

In the future, about twice as many people will retire every year in Germany than will enter the labour market for the first time. While nearly 1.4 million baby boomers were born every year between 1955 and 1970, in the years since 2000, that number has remained steady at less than 700,000 children per year. Some German regions were at almost full employment before the pandemic, and many sectors are concerned about future recruitment. In theory, Gen Zers could sit back and relax when it comes to their career plans and simply wait for demographics to shift in their favour.

The coronavirus pandemic will inevitably lead to considerable problems on the educational and labour market for the younger generation, although not all segments of Generation Z will be affected equally. The wave of digitalisation triggered by the pandemic will play into the hands of those highly qualified secondary school graduates with strong digital skills, while, in contrast, those at the weaker end of Gen Z will find it even harder to get a job. A pre-pandemic survey highlighted that 79 percent of employed under-25-year-olds stated they had found a job without difficulty – a record figure based on more than ten years of solid economic growth rates and on the fact that large numbers of workers have begun to retire.[1]

A horizon darkened by the coronavirus

The global economic crisis caused by the coronavirus has darkened career prospects for many Generation Zers. In winter 2019, 19-year-old Kurt, who is studying economics and political science in Potsdam, stated: "We think we'll all find a job, one that we enjoy." Some of Kurt's fellow students worked part-time in a bakery and earned 11 to 12 euros an hour. "Just three or four years ago, you were happy to get seven or eight euros. Now those jobs pay way above minimum wage." Of course, it is not like that everywhere, he admitted. "But you notice that the economy is good, so I've always been relaxed."

The majority of Gen Z is as optimistic about their own professional futures as they are pessimistic about the climate crisis – or at least they were until the coronavirus pandemic hit. However, despite Germany's steady economy and well-developed social safety net, the impact of twenty-first century capitalism on the country's labour market has affected the young generations the most. Not all recent graduates find traditional, permanent employment; many are hired on a temporary basis, and more and more work as freelancers for long periods, without the traditional safety mechanisms of union membership, labour protections or stable contracts. Those who only hold an intermediate, comprehensive school qualification are in a much worse position than members of Generation X and the baby boomer generation were at the same age. Those with only a basic qualification or no school-leaving certificate at all are forced to confront a very high risk of unemployment.

The labour market has shifted dramatically in the last 30 years, as incomes and job security have rapidly decreased – an instability and inequality that will continue to intensify in the wake of the coronavirus pandemic. As always in economic crises, individuals who are already employed will received the greatest support from the state, through wage subsidies, furlough schemes and corporate incentives. While the jobs held by baby boomers (aged 50 to 65), Generation Xers (35 to 50) and Generation Yers (20 to 35) are under threat, most companies will have to carefully consider whether they really want to do without their well-qualified and experienced workforce, likely opting to curtail new hires instead of losing existing staff.

The majority of Generation Z is still in school, with only the older cohorts already at university or in vocational training. Due to the strength of the economy, thus far only a few young people have had to worry about their professional futures. Very well-qualified young people will continue to have little trouble making the leap from school to professional life, but for rest of this generation, the maxim holds that the weaker the school-leaving certificate and the lower the personal qualifications, the greater the risk of being left out.

Even in less crisis-prone times, the transition from school to work has always been filled with anxiety for many young people, even the well-qualified. Carla is one of them. She wants to attend university, maybe in Berlin, and study something that earns a good salary. That is an argument in favour of becoming a psychologist, she says, rather than a kindergarten teacher, her second career choice. Psychology is already her favourite subject at school, notes the 16-year-old in a dark blue hoodie, but she is struggling with the decision. Like most of her classmates, she is generally optimistic about the future, but also a bit wary because the working world is changing faster than it has in a long time.

There have been plenty of warning signs. The powerful automobile corporations, for example, the backbone of the German economy, had already lost much of their aura of invulnerability before coronavirus through the diesel emissions scandal and the climate debate. The school closures and the pivot to online learning at the university level, along with the hesitant switch to distance learning, have also aptly demonstrated how underdeveloped digital information and communication technology is in Germany.

Young people react intuitively to these developments. In their analyses of what the future holds, they often seem closer to reality than many a manager or politician. Since 2015, the year in which it became public knowledge that Volkswagen and other German car manufacturers had circumvented emission standards with illegal cut-off devices, the industry's reputation among 15 to 24-year-olds has fallen sharply. Banks and insurance companies were hit even harder. The winners, on the other hand, were the construction industry, which has been booming for years, health care professions – with a secure future, if only because of demographic shifts in Germany – and trades.[2]

Even before the outbreak of the coronavirus, almost half of young people believed that digital technology would change their (future) professions significantly or very significantly.[3] "More and more professions are now being replaced by machines," says Carla. "That naturally makes you think about whether the job you'd like is going to exist in the future." That being said, she thinks she's on the safe side of that equation: Kindergarten teachers and psychologists won't disappear that fast, she believes. "One needs to interact individually with people. And a machine can't do that, I guess."

Risks of artificial intelligence

Generation Z's assessment is also shared by experts. In specialist and skilled occupations, half of the work could be done by machines. Even in the professional sphere, a quarter of activities previously completed by highly educated, well-paid experts could be lost to automation. While it is unlikely that a machine will replace human labour everywhere possible, millions of jobs are nonetheless potentially threatened.

"The factor that will most strongly shape the future of work is digitalisation," writes internet journalist Sascha Lobo. "And the factor that will shape digitalisation the most in the coming years is artificial intelligence."[4]

Intelligent machines are already doing things today that were long considered impossible. "Until now, if you saw a piece of writing, it was like a certificate that a human was involved in it," the US magazine *The New Yorker* quotes Dario Amodei. Amodei is research director at OpenAI, a company that researches artificial intelligence. "Now it is no longer a certificate that an actual human is involved." OpenAI is experimenting with GPT-2, the company's supercomputer, which produces text that quite convincingly matches *The New Yorker*'s literary style, including word choice, but still lacks the necessary research and context, so the text quickly drifts off into meaningless gibberish. In some newspaper editorial offices, on the other hand, computers already summarise stock market events or write the article on the latest minor league baseball game. The technical possibilities are growing rapidly: Innovations in chip design, network architecture and cloud computing have increased computer performance much faster than predicted, writes *The New Yorker*.[5]

"Education, training, the acquisition of 'human capital,' a high level of motivation and willingness to perform – all this no longer seems to be a guarantee for a professional career with an income that makes a good life possible," writes Lisa Herzog, a philosopher. "The upheaval that robots, algorithms and artificial intelligence could generate is unknown."[6]

Generation Z, however, already has experience with crises. Having pointed to the risks that the climate crisis poses to their existence for years, they should have little difficulty dealing with the rise of artificial intelligence. The segment of the younger generation we call Generation Greta is inwardly prepared to cope with uncertainty; they possess the necessary flexibility, awareness and willingness to innovate.

Although the coronavirus crisis has already changed the trajectory of the German economy and may lead to the disappearance of certain industries, it has also accelerated technological change, in particular the rise of the digital. Digitalisation is destroying jobs at the same rate it is creating new ones. This is an opportunity for Gen Zers, despite the risks involved. While older employees are more often forced to retrain at the height of their professional lives, as industries evolve or die off, young people can focus on future industries from the start of their careers. And beyond that, constant learning is already part of their everyday lives. Many companies are therefore likely to depend on their younger employees, especially in times of transformation, instead of laboriously retraining older employees.

If you ask members of Generation Z what professional and social opportunities they associate with digitalisation, they are pretty laid-back. More than 60 percent expect personal advantages.[7] Older generations, on the other hand, harbour reservations and fears; their willingness to embrace digital change is often modest.

There is no doubt that the coronavirus pandemic will significantly change the labour market in the coming years, and the need for young people to understand those structural changes will be all the more important. Even before the crisis hit, they lacked clear and well-structured information about career prospects that also took their personal situations into consideration. Schools and universities in particular have failed in this regard; only 44 percent of students felt sufficiently informed.[8] Instead, they sought advice from their parents, who have long become the go-to source, along with other family members, friends and acquaintances, as well as researching online.

The crucial role of parents in these decisions tracks with Generation Z's overall lifestyle, with many parents happy to act as personal career advisers. There are often more parents in the audiences at university open days than young people. Higher education institutions have long since set up hotlines for parents, because they make about half of all inquiries concerning study programmes and admission requirements. Companies that provide vocational training for apprentices are now also responding to this reality: Newsletters, information events, job fairs, company tours – everything is catered not only to secondary school graduates but also to their parents. Gen Zers consult their parents on all their educational decisions; the same process applies to career choice and entry into professional life. Their motto is: "Not without my parents."

The agony of choice

Although the current economic crisis may have darkened career prospects, it certainly will not change a feature typical of the transition from school to professional life: the agony of choice. Young people suffer under the weight of too many options rather than too few. Those young people who decide to go to university no longer have the choice between perhaps 300 programmes, as was the case for their parents; today, they have to search among over 12,000 bachelor's degrees to find the right one. And then beyond that, they also have to consider whether that choice is compatible with one of the 8,000 available master's degrees. In addition, these programmes are offered at various types of universities – here, too, the number of options is constantly increasing.

For almost half of all secondary school graduates in Germany who do not want to attend university, the choice is somewhat more manageable, but nevertheless includes almost 400 apprenticeships in the "dual system," a combination of practical vocational training and attendance at a vocational school. "That's a lot of pressure," says Carla. "This isn't a small decision. Your whole life depends on it."

Petra Ruthven-Murray is an island of calm in this sea of almost unlimited possibilities. Her consulting company planZ promises to "help you find your dream degree." The company advertises with successful clients like Paul, a listless, unmotivated secondary school graduate who was only interested in sports. In terms of personality, Paul was more of a tinkerer; the consultants therefore recommended he enrol in the Sports Equipment Technology programme in Vienna. Today, Paul is a doctoral student at the University of Calgary in Canada, researching the role of the brain in human movement.

"We get people who are willing to make conscious decisions," says Ruthven-Murray. Many have ideas, some seek reassurance, others need advice on which steps to take. Their consultation is geared toward the educated middle class. "Our target group simply has little experience with taking their lives into their own hands," observes Ruthven-Murray.

Ruthven-Murray first administers a series of tests to uncover the young person's personality, interests, motivations and aptitudes. Then a four to five-hour consultation follows, in which they explore various career possibilities together and she advises them on possible career paths. Most come at the beginning of their last year of school or in early summer shortly before or after getting their Abitur. Sometimes it is the young people looking for advice; sometimes, it is the parents, when they want to encourage their offspring to finally make a decision. A consultation costs 1,300 euros.

The families who seek out these services often try to outsource the decision on how to proceed after school – precisely because the relationship between parents and children is so close. "They first try to discuss it as a family. If children want to wait, parents often assume that they just want to chill out. This leads to conflict, so I outsource the conflict to the coach," says Ruthven-Murray. Some Gen Zers also just do not want to discuss this issue with their parents. "They want to finally do something on their own."

Finding one's orientation in such a crowded apprenticeship and university landscape in a multi-option society is exhausting. Many are so overwhelmed that they first take a gap year after leaving school to regroup and regain their footing. They use that year to travel around the world on their own, work here and there and think about their career prospects or courses of study.

Many parents, observes Ruthven-Murray, are concerned that their children get stuck in a holding pattern after leaving school and lose their work rhythm. "I don't think they just want to chill out," Ruthven-Murray admonishes these hypothetical parents. "I have an increasing number of young people in for consultation who are committed to the climate strike, who sacrifice their time for really important social goals. That's not chilling out."

Nevertheless, young people continue to come to her, looking for support in planning the next stages of their lives – which means that about 120 young people sit down with Ruthven-Murray year after year to go through nearly 20,000 study programmes. She herself also has to "read, read, read" to stay on top of things. Her clients are often confused by the sheer number of options, Ruthven-Murray observes. "Often a lot of things are thrown into one pot and given an incredibly fancy name," says the consultant. "But although the programme is now called media marketing, it's still a business degree, it just sounds hipper." In addition to the marketing effect, the industry reference is also meant to ensure job-related learning. "Then sometimes I get an 'oh, it's the same thing.'"

Ruthven-Murray advocates for a more relaxed approach when it comes to choosing a programme. It ultimately does not matter which field a young person chooses, perhaps with the exception of engineering, medical or law professions, she says. What really counts is having an academic degree. In more and more industries, the job market of the future will require a high degree of flexibility. For most companies, it is important that job applicants have a degree, but the degree itself is becoming less and less important. A bachelor's degree in philosophy can now lead to a successful career in human resources, and even in Germany, which is extremely conservative in this respect, government ministries no longer hire only lawyers but also economists and social scientists.

"Study anything. Show the world that you can learn." That is is the most important thing, according to Ruthven-Murray. In her experience, this takes the pressure off young people and makes them feel that this decision is not just about the name of the degree but also about other parameters: the size of the educational institution, its distance from home and whether they study at a university or a more structured university of applied science. Feel-good factors also help determine the level of success.

The ideal workplace

For Gen Z, work means self-realisation. And they are not alone in that worldview. Today's "society of singularities" enables "the self-development of individuals in a breadth and intensity unknown in classical modernity," writes Andreas Reckwitz. The sociologist has observed a "post-Romantic revolution of authenticity in the new middle class."[9] This urge to be authentic has had an unmistakable effect on the career plans of young people. After studying political science and economics in Potsdam, Kurt would like a job that also becomes his purpose in life. "I'm optimistic that I'll find a job I enjoy," says the 19-year-old. "For me, fulfilment is the main reason to do something, not earning a lot of money." The pragmatism of earlier generations has given way to a demanding and complicated personal orientation. It will be exciting to see if this can survive under coronavirus conditions.

One thing, however, is for sure: Gen Zers want to make something of their professional lives. Their chosen profession should be tailored to them, be fun, offer security, correspond to their abilities and preferences and fulfil personal needs. Self-determination and social utility are high up on the list of desires, as are personal esteem, a good working atmosphere, flat hierarchies with the ability to have a say and regular and detailed feedback. Young people want to be noticed.[10]

"Economic models assume that work is primarily a means to earn an income," writes Lisa Herzog, the philosopher, with "loftier" professions being the sole exception. "This is a preconception." Work is more than a means of earning money. The working world is "part of our common society and must also be understood as such."[11] Generation Z would agree. For them, work is part of their social lives, albeit with a clear separation between job and leisure. If they could create a workplace themselves, it would look something like this: A team of nice co-workers, a good salary, a clear-cut job description, professional development and a self-determined work schedule – and when the time comes, the opportunity to combine family and career. Most would like to have fixed working hours, and a similar number agree with the statement that it is important for them to be able to work remotely, at least some of the time.[12]

Coronavirus after-effects

The coronavirus pandemic has thrown such expectations into question overnight. Until the beginning of 2020, it looked as if the difference between Generation Z and Generation Y, who are now between 20 and 35 years old, could hardly be greater. Faced with mass unemployment at the turn of the millennium, followed by the financial crisis a few years later, Gen Yers had good reason to worry about the job market. Many shuffled from internship to internship, or from one temporary contract to the next, until they found secure permanent employment. Generation Z did not have these worries, with only one in four afraid of becoming unemployed themselves one day.[13]

The economic consequences of the pandemic have destroyed this optimism. Gen Zers with a low level of education are most at risk of unemployment, although those with average or good qualifications are also worried. That being said, the flexibility and resilience of Generation Z should not be underestimated. Developments on the job market were unpredictable before the coronavirus hit, which made Gen Zers extremely careful in planning their futures.

Gen Zers want a combination of fulfilment and security. They see that many of the dreams Generation Y entertained cannot be realised in the digital age, as work requirements continue to radically change. Relying on finding personal fulfilment only at work is too much of a stretch for them. They also do not share the Yers' visions of blurring the borders between work and life. While Generation Z also strives to combine family and career responsibilities, they want to separate their working lives from their private lives with clear, distinct structures, as opposed to the open model favoured by Generation Y.

This mindset applies especially to young women. While the women of Generation Y still place specific materialistic and social demands on their careers and want to reconcile work and family life, young Gen Z women, despite their professional ambitions, place their faith in a good partnership and do not want to experiment with the pressure of managing both roles, which is also why they are more inclined toward a classic division of labour. Following the birth of a child, Generation Z expects the woman to only work part-time and take on most of the parenting responsibilities.[14] Young women and men agree on this point, which is astonishing, given the enormous strides that girls have made in access to education and vocational training in the last 20 years, not to mention that almost all young women today invest a great deal of time and energy in launching their professional careers. This gendered division of labour experienced a resurgence during the coronavirus pandemic.

Here too, Generation Z seem to copy their parents as role-models, even more as they see how difficult it still is for women to reconcile family life and a successful career. Most companies hesitate to allow flexible working hours for mothers or fathers (despite the fact that, in Germany, there is a law on the books that makes such arrangements available to most employees under certain conditions), and in many European countries there is a notorious lack of day-cares, nurseries and all-day schools. When schools closed because of the pandemic, it was once again women who shouldered the double burden of work and family responsibilities to a much larger extent.

A safeguard against burnout

Nicholas's stress levels really began to climb during his first semester at university. "That's when I noticed that I let myself go a little because studying was so exhausting," the physics student recalls. Less exercise, eating less, less time for friends and family – he never wants to experience that again. "Of course, it's important to me to have a good job," he says. "But it's much more important that I'm plugged into myself and my environment." This choice was quite different for his parents, he says. "Especially with my father, I saw how he was always focused on work." His father took early retirement, and his parents are separated.

With the arrival of Generation Z, a critical generation is entering the job market. Many are not willing to compromise, even under increasingly difficult conditions on the labour market. Employers are well advised to listen carefully to them, even if their complaints seem overly demanding and self-centred. In the era of round-the-clock availability, Generation Zers do not want to be overworked, stressed or taken advantage of – they are very concerned about the toll it can take on their health. They are afraid of burning out, and therefore do not hesitate to ask for breaks and time off. Managers need to accept this and maintain constant contact with their young co-workers and react immediately to criticism, especially in the arena of mental and physical health. If they feel personally addressed and understood, young employees are quite willing to agree to certain arrangements in cooperation with their employers.[15]

Working from such a perspective, it is surprising that Generation Z still lists the non-material aspects of professional life at the top of their priorities when looking for a job. As a rule, the money has to be right, but it is not everything. They cannot be lured with high salaries if all their other workplace expectations are not met. Even special incentives such as a company car or free access to a gym are only valued if they really are an expression of appreciation and not perceived as a cheap pick-up line.[16]

Vocational training – A losing battle

Frank Bätje trains budding carpenters, but today he is making candlesticks with eighth-grade students at the Magdeburg Chamber of Commerce and Trade vocational training centre. They may be the skilled workers of tomorrow, but they still have difficulty drilling a hole in the middle of a 40-centimetre-wide board. "That isn't the centre," Bätje explains patiently after taking the necessary measurements. "On one side, we have 16 cm, and on the other 24."

"Since 1900, the crafts and manual skills trades have only ever experienced one thing: I could open the door and young people would be standing there, wanting to learn my profession," says Viola Keuters, head of the vocational training centre. "Now, it's different." Within five years, the number of apprentices has dropped by half. "That shows you how dramatic the situation has become."

It is a turning point for Germany's hailed vocational training system. Many consider vocational training a key to the success of the country's economy in the twentieth century. In-house training provides the hands-on experience, and the accompanying lessons at the vocational school provide the theoretical foundation. Students sign an employment contract and earn their own money from the very first day. They are often kept on permanently after finishing their apprenticeship – one major reason why youth unemployment is lower in Germany than anywhere else in Europe. But for years now, the appeal of vocational training has been on the decline. Instead, Generation Z is increasingly pinning its hopes on a bachelor's or master's degree. For decades, significantly more young people in Germany began an apprenticeship instead of attending university. Since 2013, that relationship has been turned on its head; today, more young people enrol at university than sign an apprenticeship contract.[17]

Traditional vocational training – a system that has won Germany international admiration – has lost its prestige for Generation Z. Fewer apprentices, a smaller number of companies (around 20 percent) that still provide training – this trend is likely to continue in response to the coronavirus crisis, which has shuttered many small businesses. Generation Z is experiencing the radical shift in professional qualifications first hand. In addition, the decline in young people starting an apprenticeship has coincided with a growing lack of qualified specialists – a problem faced by many European economies.

More and more chambers of commerce and trade associations have therefore begun to operate inter-company training facilities. At the Magdeburg Vocational Training Centre, 150 kilometres west of Berlin, two dozen 14-year-old comprehensive school students are bent over their assigned vices. "I'm cutting a threaded rod for my clamp," says Christopher. "A vocational orientation like this is a good thing for later," says Christopher's classmate Paul. "But I'm also doing an internship and stuff. I'm trying to find out what I can do best." Paul has already completed two days of intro courses with the painters and varnishers. He liked the fact that he could let his imagination run free, he says. But he also really enjoys working with metal.

In order to win over Generation Zers, the Magdeburg Chamber of Commerce and Trade initiated a project offering a practice-oriented transition from school to training. Metalworker is the fourth profession Paul has tried out. "I still have two years to go," he says. "Then I'll decide what I want to do." The choice: Continue at school until he has his Abitur or take on an apprenticeship, which he could start earlier. In the past, apprenticeships were almost a matter of course for comprehensive school students. The Chamber of Commerce and Trade has also observed the large advisory role played by parents when it comes to the choice of occupation – with mixed feelings. In response to digitalisation, job descriptions are currently undergoing fundamental changes, Viola Keuters points out. "Today's metalworker is not the same metalworker that Dad was," says Keuters. "It's a completely different job description. More modern, you have lots of opportunities."

Workers swarm the 70-metre high towers right next to Hanover's main train station like ants on an anthill. The headquarters of Sparkasse Hanover, a regional bank, is undergoing a complete renovation, and several companies are onsite at the same time. Schubert GmbH, an electric company, has been tasked with the electrical work: Power connections, motion sensors and electricity for a total area of 36,000 square metres. The bank building renovation is only one of the many major construction projects on the books of this medium-size company from the small village of Tangerhütte near Magdeburg. The business, with branches in Hamburg and Wismar, employs 180 people – but it could be more.

Companies that want to stay in this business need skilled workers. But highly qualified electricians are hard to find on the open market, says Volker Schubert, the managing director. "If we advertise in a big daily newspaper, we might get one application." He regularly submits job vacancies to the local unemployment office: "Zero. Not a single application." The company's training manager Sandra Raebel believes that "we have to be more creative and offer our apprentices something more." And equally important, when potential apprentices come to test out how much they like working at the company, the message has to be clear: "Electricians can't be downsized." On the contrary, digitalisation will ultimately create more work for them, as more and more apartment buildings and houses are retrofitted to become digitally controlled smart buildings – something that will hopefully motivate Generation Z to choose the profession.

The dual life of a dual-track programme

Markus is trying to find a ladder among the hustle and bustle of the Sparkasse construction site in Hanover; he has been working here as an apprentice with Schubert GmbH for nine months. His job today is to connect the control boxes mounted to the ceiling of the third floor, which is why he needs the ladder. "The box I'm working on here costs 600 euros," explains Markus. "And here on this floor alone we have 60 boxes, so you can imagine how much money is behind all this." Markus is not only an apprentice, but also a student. In addition to working part-time at the construction site, he is studying electrical engineering part-time at the University of Magdeburg. He will also complete a full-time paid internship year with the company. Getting paid to study – that is how Schubert GmbH retains young people long-term and actively attempts to minimise the company's skilled labour shortage.

The dual-track programme is an attempt by businesses and government to offset the deficit of highly skilled, specialist labour. Due to the continuous coordination between education institution and company, dual-track students receive much more practical training than if they were exclusively enrolled at traditional technical colleges or universities. On the flipside, they also receive a higher level of theoretical training than if they had only signed up for a traditional apprenticeship. Thousands of German companies have already gained experience with this type of dual-track system, and, in many cases, companies have even taken the initiative to reach out to the universities and vocational colleges themselves.

"To us, the dual student is first and foremost a student," says Markus's boss, Volker Schubert. But unlike an ordinary student, Markus knows his trade inside out. For companies like Schubert GmbH, the advantage here is retaining young people at an early stage of their working lives. "When a student finishes a regular study programme, he or she won't go to a mid-sized company," says Schubert. "There are too many major corporations waiting in line that would gladly take them on." But "his" students are already employees at his company, making the dual study programme an attractive and mutually beneficial means of ensuring the next generation of Schubert employees.

Generation Z loves this educational model, and no other has grown as rapidly in Germany in recent years, from around 50,000 students in 2009 to 125,000 in 2020. This is the answer for many young people to changes in the labour market. They appreciate the interconnection between the practical and the theoretical. Demand for such dual-track programmes is particularly strong in finance and economics, engineering and computer science, but degree courses in the social and health sectors and in administration and public service have also proven to be very attractive.

Once all the connection boxes at the construction site in Hanover have been wired, Markus returns to the office. He documents his work himself. As a dual student, he is constantly changing roles, he says. "One day, I won't be on the construction site as a fitter – I'll work as a site manager and project manager."

Not all young people have what it takes, like Markus does, for such a demanding course of study. For those who graduate from school after nine years with a poor basic qualification, the chance of even getting into a traditional apprenticeship program is slim. In Germany, this segment encompasses about a fifth of all young people, most of whom come from socially disadvantaged homes. And year after year, almost seven percent of all students in Germany continue to leave school without a degree at all. Socially marginalised, they clearly are in a precarious position and often feel frustrated because they know that their performance cannot keep up with the majority of their peers.[18] Conversely, there are regions in Germany where companies are desperately seeking apprentices and future employees. The hopes of such companies, as well as the hopes of many disadvantaged young people, rest on people like Dirk Petri. The social worker and his team supervise apprentices as part of an assisted training programme. "This programme gives me the chance to find young people who don't necessarily correspond 100 percent to a company's ideas and still give them a chance," Petri explains the appeal of the initiative.

Tobias is one of them. He works as a normal apprentice; Dirk Petri only steps in with support when he has problems. He can also apply for extra tutoring for the vocational school he attends. "The work day is orderly, precise – neat and tidy," says the 24-year-old and adds with a smile: "We start on time." The smile reveals that he still finds it hard to get up early; the company even set up a wake-up service for him.

Tobias was unemployed for three years before he was accepted into the assisted training programme. Petri and his team analysed his talents, then Tobias participated in trial assignments at several companies. "The longer you're unemployed, the longer it takes to get used to going back to work. It is also more difficult to get back into the swing of things."

The call he was waiting for came on a weekend. "They found a place for me after all, which made me really, really happy." So far, his boss is satisfied: "We still have to work on the discipline a bit," says Gerhard Kleve. "But that's part of normal life, and it's not a problem for the time being" – because Tobias is good at his job.

Many disadvantaged young people are extremely impressed by such a personal and targeted approach. They have, after all, never had another person or institution show such an interest in them or the willingness to work with them. If successful, it can lead to close cooperation and long-standing working relationships.

A university degree is the norm

It's time for debriefing after morning rounds at the psychiatric clinic in Teupitz, south of Berlin. Chief physician Stefan Kropp takes the time to check in with the two medical students who are currently studying on his ward. Mania, depression, alcohol abuse – they discuss the morning's cases over a cup of coffee in Kropp's chic office. "You have to watch out for them," says Kropp. "You have to let them know that they are welcome here and that they can learn something while they are here."

Hospitals used to be known for exploiting medical residents with gruelling 24-hour shifts. Some assistant doctors even worked full-time – while signed up to part-time contracts. Today, the situation has changed: Many hospitals – especially in rural areas – often receive only one or two applications in response to job advertisements. Germany has more doctors than ever before, says Kropp, "but even more are needed to care for an ageing population, and there are currently not enough students who choose to study medicine."

At medical conferences, there is always talk of young colleagues who either want to work guaranteed eight-hour shifts or reduce their hours to 80 percent. This leads to a lot of headshaking among the older generation of doctors – many of whom were working 16 hours in a row at that age – or respect, since almost everyone there has been on the verge of burnout at some point. Today, if a clinic or hospital does not meet the expectations of junior staff, they will simply move on.

The tuition-paying students at Szczecin University know this, too. The lights have been turned off in the seminar room and a projector beams a diagram of a human arm onto the screen. At two long tables, about 30 young people eagerly take notes.

By deciding to enrol at university, the majority of Gen Zers are – above all – giving themselves access to a greater number of options later. Higher education creates more opportunities – that is the logic. Greater access to knowledge also helps them to better assess shifts in the working world, which is another reason why the younger generation – more women than men – is flocking to universities.

Shaping digital change

Digitalisation and globalisation – the trends that will decisively shape the professional lives of Generation Z – are often described as unstoppable processes that cannot be regulated, according to philosopher Lisa Herzog. "But if politics and civil society do nothing to shape digital change, then others will step in."[19]

Gen Zers want to shape these tectonic shifts. They are young and the majority are not yet gainfully employed. The activists among them, the members of Generation Greta, are already engaged in lively discussions on how to transform the economy in the face of the climate crisis at local Fridays for Future meetings. Similarly, digital change is also on their agenda, as demonstrated by the protests against upload filters online, which they fear will restrict their creativity and freedom of expression in the name of protecting the copyrights of wealthy corporations. Half of the young generation is certain that digitalisation will change practically everything about their careers and adult lives. At the same time, a majority is optimistic that these changes will help them find professional opportunities.

Their most pressing concern, however, remains the climate crisis. Companies that continue to rely on fossil fuels in their production and service provision will have significantly more difficulty recruiting and retaining this generation of workers than those that preceded it. In the eyes of young people, the climate is a measure of how well companies are prepared for the future, and that long-term sustainability will be crucial for them as they go about choosing a career.[20]

Without new talent, it will become increasingly difficult for major corporations and mid-size companies to remain innovative in the era of digitalisation. The demographic powerlessness that Generation Z often feels when confronted with political structures controlled by their elders is in sharp contrast to the demographic power they are able to assert within the economy. When the baby boomers retire, few companies will be able to do without the youngest generation, and the wave of digitalisation caused by the coronavirus pandemic will certainly accelerate this.

This is the reality not only for large corporations, but small and mid-sized ones as well. In Brandenburg, near Berlin, nurseries and landscaping companies report that their apprentices are calling into question whether they really need to memorise the general appearance of over 200 plant species and their leaves when they could easily identify them with the help of their smartphones and programmes like Google Lens. They can learn the most common species on the job and leave the rest to technology – easily done since they always have their phones in their pockets anyways. Companies are thus well advised to secure such young, digitally inclined talents even when the economic outlook is still shaky. In the long run, their presence will pay off, especially when the company teams them up with older employees. While 50 to 65-year-old colleagues from the baby boomer generation are able to reflect endurance and reliability, the young people stand for speed and digital multitasking. Older employees can show the younger ones how to persevere in difficult situations and bring a boring job to an end; younger employees can inspire and motivate older generations with their digital curiosity and openness.

As a whole, Generation Z is invested in demanding that companies recognise their social and ecological responsibilities. They want to experience being part of a community at work and would like to see companies practise their social commitment by supporting kindergartens, retirement homes and environmental protection initiatives. They want a place of employment that is social and humane, especially in times of crisis.

Notes

1 Köcher et al. 2019, p. 92.
2 Köcher et al. 2019, p. 65.
3 Köcher et al. 2019, p. 47.
4 Lobo 2019, p. 220.
5 Seabrook 2019.
6 Herzog 2019, p. 7.
7 Köcher et al. 2019, p. 44.
8 Köcher et al. 2019, p. 80.
9 Reckwitz 2018, p. 19 ff.
10 Köcher et al. 2019, p. 60.
11 Herzog 2019, p. 12.
12 Leven et al. 2019b, p. 191.
13 Köcher et al. 2019, p. 13.
14 Wolfert and Quenzel 2019, p. 148.
15 Köcher et al. 2019, p. 58.
16 Köcher et al. 2019, p. 78.
17 Autorengruppe Bildungsberichterstattung 2018, p. 140.
18 Autorengruppe Bildungsberichterstattung 2018, p. 121.
19 Herzog 2019, p. 19.
20 Köcher et al. 2019, p. 47.

Chapter 11

The private lives of Generation Greta

Gender, sexuality and relationships

From hetero to LGBTQI*

On the day that will change his life, Max is sitting in the stairwell of Sophie Scholl Secondary School in Berlin, looking at the screen of his phone. Suddenly, a classmate grabs it out of his hand – which is not really the issue; the issue is that Max was scrolling through pictures of boys his age. The news that he is gay quickly spreads around the school.

The story is fictional and was developed by students at the school for a video project. Nevertheless, it will be a long road for "Max" until the title of the short film proves true: "Gay is okay." He is in the process of considering a school transfer when his classmates suddenly apologise to him. "Thanks to you, we realised that what we did wasn't right," one of them says and adds, "We realised that everyone is different." Admittedly, the transformation comes as a bit of a surprise at the end, but the five-minute video won third place in an anti-discrimination short film festival in Berlin and Brandenburg.

Head teacher Juliane Westphal observes more tolerance for other sexual identities at her school than four or five years ago. "Some students come out officially," she says. Others wear nail polish or other markers of their queer identity. "That's perfectly okay and totally accepted." There has been a notable shift in how the diversity of sexual orientations is regarded: Being gay is actually okay for large segments of the younger generation. Only nine percent of those under 25 say it would bother them if a homosexual couple moved in next door.[1] For them, it is part of everyday life that people, regardless of their gender, love who they love and express their identities however they see fit.

"It's important that the older generation, which has suppressed all this, also says it's okay," demands Erin, who goes to school in Giessen. "It's okay to want to be a woman or to want to be a man. That's the human right to the free development of one's personality." Her mother told her it does not matter whether she falls in love with a woman or a man. "I'm surprised that there are people who still think it's terrible – because it's just love."

Nearly every youth magazine regularly publishes articles about LGBTQI* individuals. While the term refers to any lesbian, gay, bisexual, transsexual, queer or intersexual person, as well as individuals who do not identify with any of these labels, "queer" is often used within the community as a comprehensive term for all types of non-heteronormative sexuality and identity. Reading through Generation Z online magazines and internet platforms, it seems that a relationship with several partners, be it an open relationship or polyamory, is a valid alternative to the classic monogamous two-person model. And when Erin's mother tells her it does not matter whom she loves one day, it means above all that she has a choice. She is no longer permanently set on a heterosexual way of life and, unlike previous generations, can shape her intimate relationships according to her own personal feelings and desires.

Generation Z is harvesting the fruits of the enormous struggles for the human rights of queer people. It took decades before homosexuality was no longer punishable by law, and then further decades before same-sex partnerships were no longer merely tolerated but fully recognised – including in Germany. It was not until July 2017 that German president Frank-Walter Steinmeier signed a law opening the institution of marriage to everyone. Nonetheless, in several European countries, homosexual and non-binary people are still stigmatised and under threat.

In most Western European countries, long-cultivated prejudices and discrimination are gradually fading among Generation Zers. Many heterosexual men have also lost their reservations: Jack, who moved to Berlin from Great Britain after the Brexit referendum, enjoys attending Berlin's "voguing balls" (originally part of the queer subculture of 1980's New York) with his girlfriend; unsolicited, Kurt from Eberswalde raves about Christopher Street Day in Berlin. "For us, it's a kind of event," says the 19-year-old. "We go because it's a cool, cosmopolitan atmosphere. We walked around and talked to a lot of people." He said it was just cool to be there. "That line 'Are you gay or what?' – in my generation, I've seldom experienced that as an accusation." And Jakob in Ludwigsburg defines himself as queer. Although he has thus far only been attracted to women, the 25-year-old says that he no longer wants to limit himself mentally.

Precisely this limitation still felt necessary to many heterosexual young men 20 years ago. Despite their general tolerance, they kept their distance from the subculture of their gay friends and were careful not to raise questions about their own sexuality, either to themselves or others.

Today this worry seems to have vanished. Young – heterosexual – people declare almost unanimously that it would no longer be a problem for them to come out as gay, lesbian or queer. Many have queer classmates. In general, acceptance of the diversity of sexualities and sexual expressions has increased among adolescents and young adults in recent years.

Of course, the vast majority of Generation Z is attracted to the opposite sex and most are looking for classic one-on-one relationships and not ménages à trois or one-night stands facilitated by dating apps. As in previous generations, 90 percent define themselves as heterosexual. But the new openness creates more opportunities to try out different sexual identities, redefine gender roles or construct relationships differently. Most of the younger generation see this as an opportunity, even if not everyone wants to take advantage of it themselves.

The search for belonging and harmony

"Trust is very important," says Lilli when asked about what she thinks is important in a relationship. "Everything else follows automatically from that." The 18-year-old from Frankfurt an der Oder is currently in her second steady relationship. Her boyfriend is 23. "I've never been so sure about anything as I am about this right now."

Her classmate Lara is single again. She has always had bad luck with boys, she explains. Most of them were very into sports, but her interest lies in music. "If you're too different, that's not good either." For her, a partner has to be able to listen when she tells him about her problems and has to share his problems with her, as well. "And if, on top of that, he's cute, too…"

Most Gen Zers experience their "first time" at the age of 15, usually preceded by falling in love for the first time and some form of erotic contact beginning around the age of 12, but usually without sexual intercourse. A good third is in a steady relationship at age 18 and a half, though more young women than men have a partner by age 22.[2]

Although the younger generation is constantly exposed to a variety of relationships in the media, the majority of them – like Lilli and Lara – want to experience romantic love and harmony with a partner in a more traditional relationship. "If it's right, it's right, and if not, it's not," says Lilli. With her boyfriend it is right: "I can talk to him about anything. I want to be me around him."

Lara definitely wants to marry. "In a pure white wedding dress with a nice low-cut back, tight-fitting." In real life, Lara is wearing a loose, yellow knit sweater and a nose ring. Her dyed black hair puts her somewhere between punk and goth. "Talk about weddings and I'm all girl. I know, I want to be a bit princess-y." Using dating apps to find a partner, or even a one-night stand, is something Lara rejects as much as open relationships. "No way," she says. "Definitely not my thing."

Indeed, most young men and women yearn for the harmony and sense of belonging of a partnered relationship. As pragmatic as Generation Z is in other respects, family is important to them. It gives them stability, but also meaning. For the majority, this naturally includes the desire to have children of their own. Seventy-one percent of girls and women in Germany between the ages of 12 and 25 want to have children, compared to 64 percent of young men.[3] These values have not changed in the last 15 years. Then as now, more young women than men want to have children. Young men are rather hesitant; for them, other goals than having children come first, especially vocational training and employment. That being said, they do not question the idea of family, either. Lilli has long since decided with her boyfriend on what a family should look like. "The subject always comes up at dinner when you don't know what to talk about." Lilli would like three children; her boyfriend would like one and then to adopt another. "Sometimes, it's really obvious that we have different ideas." But these differences can be bridged, she is sure of that. The desire to have children depends heavily on how well young people get along with their own parents: The better their relationship, the more likely they are to want a family themselves. Another important factor is the level of education: The higher the level of education attained or aspired to by young people, the greater their desire to start a family.[4]

"I want to have my first child at 22," says Lilli. Her mother also had her at that age. "We have such a good relationship. She's also my best friend because the age difference isn't so huge." This is exactly what she wants for her own children.

Life with the parents

When Lilli talks about her mother, she talks about "my mummy." Clearly, the times in which young people were embarrassed by their parents are very much over. Forty-two percent of 12 to 25-year-olds in Germany state about their parents, "We get along very well with each other." A further 50 percent get on well with their parents, even if there are occasional differences of opinion. The proportion of those who are satisfied with their relationship to their parents has continuously increased in recent years.[5] Parents are Gen Z's most important role models. When this generation talks about their families, they say things like, "What would you be without your family?" or "family goes without saying" or even "in the past, parents were stricter." "It's important to me that he also gets along with my family," says Lara about her ideal partner. "My mother says I'm a difficult person, I need someone who understands me and is perhaps calmer than I am to balance me out." For the most part, Generation Z lives under the same roof as their parents, which is further evidence of the positive relationship between parents and children. Their first sexual experiences take place at home, often with the consent of their parents, who support their children as they figure out their relationships, frequently acting as advisers and speaking openly with them about their own love lives.

It is especially significant that Generation Z likes how their parents raised them. In 2019, 74 percent responded that they would bring up their children exactly as their parents had looked after them. In 1985, only 53 percent shared that opinion.[6] These figures show the close and harmonious relationship that the majority of the younger generation shares with their parents.

Despite all this harmony, there are clear differences based on social background. Approval is particularly strong among young people whose parents have high levels of education level and a well-paying job. Among them, as many as 86 percent say that they would adopt the parenting style of their own parents, compared to only 51 percent of those who grew up in the least socially advantageous circumstances.[7] This percentage is reduced even further when the young people are themselves unemployed. The lower the social status of the parents, the more likely there are to be serious tensions and misunderstandings in the relationship with their Gen Z children. These are often exacerbated by financial problems, cramped living conditions and a lack of available parental support at key moments – from preparing for school to cultivating friendships and coping with heartbreak.

For the vast majority of Gen Z, however, the close relationship with their parents even has an impact on their leisure activities. Meeting with friends and peers remains a perennially popular activity, but, in the past 15 years, its importance has declined slightly because young people are spending more and more time with their families. Indeed, almost a quarter of Generation Zers report time spent with their families as the most frequent activity in a normal week.[8] A unique feature of this development is that more and more parents find it entirely normal to go on holiday with their 20 or 30-year-old children. Gone are the days when parents were proud that they could convince their 16-year-old children to go on holiday with them one last time. Until the 1980s, being a good parent meant giving children their own space. Family holidays made way for Interrail trips alone or with friends, as mums and dads waved from the train platform, eager to have the house to themselves again and to see their children spread their wings. Today things are different, partially for economic reasons. Generation Zers have established a strategic alliance with their parents, which allows them to remain carefree "children" until the age of 30. They use this time to test out what they want to do with their lives. A third of 22 to 25-year-olds still live with their parents; they are happy to enjoy the comforts of home for as long as possible and are in no hurry to move out. On the flipside, parents are usually happy to accept this situation, with both sides striving for a relaxed relationship in the home. The motivation to continue living at "Hotel Mum & Dad" is understandable. Not only are parents protective of their children and have enjoyed spoiling them from an early age, which makes the offer of living at home easy to accept, they are also much more tolerant and open-minded, which makes it easy for Gen Zers to accept their advice on life and love. Life at home is comfortable, easy on the wallet and does not require a foray outside known comfort zones. The downside is that personal independence can fall by the wayside. Young people lack the experience in managing their own households and making responsible decisions on their own – an issue that affects young men in particular. They remain at home longer; 12 percent still live with their parents at the age of 30, even if they are employed, earn their own money and are in a long-term relationship – in contrast to only five percent of women.[9]

A traditional life with the kids

"I wouldn't want to sit at home every day and take care of the house and the kids." When Lilli imagines life with her own children, she rejects the traditional division of labour. "Both should be able to do whatever they want." It worked for her parents. "They both work. We eat dinner together every night and go on family outings on the weekends."

It will be a while before the majority of Gen Zers have their own children, especially since everything has to be perfect first. A stable relationship, a completed degree or apprenticeship, a secure job and a suitable flat – not an easy feat, given the difficult housing market – all have to be in place before they take the plunge, which is why currently young people, on average, have their first child at the age of 30. Lilli, who would like to have her first child at 22, is an exception, as is the fact that she would also like to work after that child arrives.

The percentage of employed mothers in Germany has risen continuously in recent years, although the country remains very conservative in this respect compared with other European countries. Not until 2013 was a historic trend reversed: For the first time, both parents were employed in the majority of families; before that, the classic single-income family dominated. In comparison, in the UK, currently 75 percent of mothers of underage children are employed, and in 2000, two-thirds of mothers worked.[10] In Germany, in most families, the fathers work full-time and the mothers part-time. Here too, Generation Z is following in their parents' footsteps. A minority believes in sharing the responsibilities of child-rearing and maintaining professional careers, while the majority follows a more traditional pattern. Only eight percent of young women want to work full-time once they have children; for men, that figure is 41 percent, although most ultimately do. As a rule, this does not cause conflict, as young men and women agree that women should remain at home with the children.[11] Surprisingly, young women have an even more traditional idea of fatherhood than the men themselves: The man should remain the family's main breadwinner – even if the woman also works.

While German Zers stick to traditional patterns, UK's Generation Z seems to be more attuned to gender equality. In a YouGov study only 26 percent of men aged 18 to 24 feel they need to be the main breadwinner in their (future) family, compared to more than 40 percent in older age groups.[12] At the same time, youth in both countries look to their parents in search of role models for how to live their own family lives, even if they do not adopt all details of their way of life.

These attitudes among young people reflect the prevailing social patterns, which is unexpected. For over 20 years, young women have been overtaking their male counterparts in educational achievement; young women now do better than men in most school subjects and are conquering highly respected academic professions such as medicine, law and psychology. They have accumulated masses of educational capital, which sooner or later they could exchange for career capital. And yet, despite taking over professions formerly closed to them, many women lag behind men once they start a family. As long as it remains difficult or even impossible to combine having a family and career, nothing will change. Germany lacks a suitable infrastructure to ease the burden of childrearing and maintaining a household, and companies lack the willingness to respond flexibly to the needs of employees with children.

The only question is how long Gen Z women remain content with the status quo. Women invest a lot of time and effort into developing their skills, abilities and careers. It is hard to imagine that these strong young women, so committed to a revolution in climate policy, will shy away from a revolution in family policy.

Insecure men

"You often notice that 17 or 18-year-old guys are still very immature," says Lilli. Lara has had a few boyfriends, now exes, that age. "They behave like 13-year-old boys just starting puberty." Both girls are only 18 years old themselves, but it is a well-known phenomenon that boys trail girls both physically and cognitively in their development through adolescence. Boys are also finding it increasingly difficult to find their own roles in society: For Generation Z, success is increasingly female. In school and at university, young women have long attained better qualifications – but that does not mean that all is well. "Sexism is still an issue," says Pia. "Women still earn less than men, and that bothers me." They also have to do more to have a successful career. Indeed, social workers still work specifically with girls to strengthen their self-esteem and self-assertion skills.

Nevertheless, the 14-year-old from Giessen is optimistic that, as a woman, she will herself not suffer any disadvantages. "I think this will also continue to improve." Girls have expanded their roles in society and are considering occupations that were once male strongholds, from the armed forces to the media, from theatre and culture to football and politics. In contrast, young men are hesitant to expand their own options. Most of them do not see any advantages to entering female-dominated professions. They receive little encouragement from their social environment to become more emotional and communicative, and experience considerable rejection from their peers at school if they attempt to develop in that direction.[13]

Lilli and Lara want to become early childhood educators. "I think men have a hard time in this profession because of all the prejudices," says Lilli. But men are very important as early childhood educators and teachers to provide boys with vital role models from the very start.

Beginning with their first romper in pink or blue, young people are constantly and continually confronted with clichéd patterns of masculinity and femininity – not least in the media. Traditional femininity in Germany is most often based on physical attractiveness and appropriate feminine behaviour, while masculinity is based on dominance, recognition by male peers and female admiration. How parents raise their children – whether consciously or unconsciously – is often still based on gender-specific norms and ideals. Teachers also have different expectations for the girls and boys in their classrooms.

At the same time, young people today have a real opportunity to (re-) define their own gender roles. But in order to do so, they have to confront the expectations set not only by their parents and grandparents but by society's clichéd gender norms. This applies as much to young heterosexual people as to the minority of young people with other sexual identities. While young women are generally more flexible in dealing with the heavy social and individual demands of adolescence, young men often cling to biased and traditional understandings of masculinity. They are afraid to expand the traditional role of men in society – which emphasises work, making money and building a career – to include other facets of life that still carry a female connotation: children, the home and community.

Young men's reluctance to embrace all aspects of life in a society can be explained as a lack of willingness to cope with the demands of the twenty-first century, although in recent years an increasing number of them have followed the trend towards a more flexible division of labour. Well-educated individuals in particular realise that they are headed for a dead end if they keep holding on to traditional gender roles.

Society has changed. In the age of digitalisation, communication skills are essential, and, in the age of individualisation, social skills and empathy count. Self-management and self-discipline are becoming increasingly important. More and more young men are becoming aware of these new realities and are gradually beginning to expand the traditional features of male gender roles. An indication of this trend is that half of male adolescents today think that it is important to be able to work part-time once they have children. Approval rates are even higher for the statement that family and children should not be neglected when pursuing a career.[14]

Love online

Gen Zers express their love online, and the romantic overtures they employ to court their first loves are often not that different from those whispered by older generations over the phone: a kiss or heart emoji via text message. As in any other relationship today, WhatsApp and Co. also play a role in maintaining the connection to one's partner(s).

But the internet, of course, can do much more. "My best friend, he likes to check out girls on Lovoo," says Katherina, 18 years old. The dating portal advertises with the tagline "For one night, for a few months, perhaps for a lifetime. Whatever you are looking for, we give you the chance to find it." "He says that he wants to experiment to the fullest and doesn't want a steady girlfriend." He just does not feel ready yet. "Then he swipes through the profiles and says, 'Okay, maybe I could write to that one.'"

But Katherina and her classmate Sophie are sceptical. "I wouldn't meet a stranger to have sex with him," Sophie says. "I couldn't do that. I need to have feelings for someone." Plus, you never know who you are going to meet online. "I think these dating apps are just a way to get laid and not a way to find a steady relationship," Katherina says. That is probably why her best friend has so much success with the apps – the girls who sign up are also usually not looking for something permanent.

For young people, the "first time" has always been full of expectations and probably a little fear. They see the ability to freely determine their sexual behaviour as an expression of emancipation and maturity. "For boys and girls, the loss of virginity means that they can join the social class of sexually desirable people," writes Eva Illouz, a sociologist. Sex thus also becomes a sort of social capital. According to Illouz, the internet has transformed casual sex into a commodity as dating apps make the organisation of sexual encounters in a virtual marketplace possible and accessible.[15] "There are boys, but also girls, who want to experiment and see how it works before they get into a relationship," observes Katherina. Others are looking for a distraction after a break-up. "Then, you take what you can't get from the person you've been with for years anymore, so that you don't have to be alone."

"There was this girl," says Anna about an incident at her old school. "Someone sent a nude picture of her around on social media. First to one person, then to someone else, and so on. It really made the rounds." Anna's story is an example of what happens when sexting goes wrong. "You just want to crawl into a hole and die when something like that happens," adds the 17-year-old. In her class, many of her friends report that they have witnessed material of a sexual nature circulating online among their contacts. Most of these messages are sexually suggestive text messages, but photos and clips are becoming increasingly common on digital platforms. Katherina's best friend is also into sexting. "He also tells me when he exchanges naked pictures with a friend," she says, "He brags about it to me." She says she does not care. "If he wants to talk about it, let him talk about it."

Revenge porn has been widely discussed as a phenomenon in the press in the United States and the United Kingdom. Many young people are not aware of the enormous risks they take when they take photos of themselves naked or exposed and send them to others – especially when pictures exchanged willingly during a relationship are sent around after a break-up to hurt their (usually female) ex. According to media reports, there have been incidents in which girls committed suicide because they could not deal with the public attention and comments associated with the pictures.

Studies show that mainly the sexually active segment of Generation Z engages in sexting. Getting to know one's body and learning how to engage with intimacy are a major part of adolescent identity development and reflect the desire to establish close relationships, experience one's own body and an intimacy that can lead to a sexual interaction. In such a context, sexting can be a stimulating activity and a sign of connection, familiarity and mutual attraction. It becomes a psychosocial problem when young people engage in sexting outside consenting relationships or when they feel pressured to participate by a partner or their peers. The social context determines whether sexting is a fun act of bonding, a symptom of sexual insecurity or an act of sexual aggression.

Since the 1960s, the social rules around love, sex and relationships have expanded greatly but never resulted in such disengaged relationship patterns as we see today. The vast majority of Generation Z sees sex as an integral but not particularly important part of a romantic relationship and want to make their own decisions about it based on their own standards and desires in the moment. The same applies to pornography, which parallels the trends in sexting. The vast majority of young people deal with pornographic material in a conscious manner and actively seek out the porn that interests them personally online. The situation becomes critical when group pressure affects this self-determination and goads them into consuming degrading, discriminatory or violent material, which can lead to personality disorders, the development of deleterious behavioural patterns and damaging relationships in real life. Unwanted contact with pornography sent out in bulk messages, for example via chat groups at school, is also highly problematic, because younger kids are developmentally unready to understand or categorise what they see.

Loving differently

A ringtone. About a dozen young adults – both men and women – sit around a table at the Youth Community Centre in Freiburg and play charades. An outsider would feel clueless, wondering how one player immediately guessed "Goethe" just from the ringtone, but it causes great amusement among the group. The industrial fluorescent ceiling lights have been dimmed, and a red-blue lamp shines softly from one corner throughout the room. The Rosekids, a gay and lesbian youth group, meet here every Wednesday and Friday. The group has been around for 25 years. Today, the letters "BI" in the word "lesBIan" are printed in bold in the organisation's name. No sexual orientation is excluded, their website claims. "Whatever you are, feel free to drop by whenever you like!"

An estimated ten percent of young people are attracted to members of the same sex. Another two to three percent are attracted to both men and women. A small number identify as non-binary or tend to call themselves queer, transsexual or intersexual.

For Daniel and Julien, the Rosekids were the logical next step after coming out. "I started to ask myself: What are you going to do with your sexuality? How do you want to live it? What kind of people do you want to meet?" Julien says, sitting in a smaller quiet room at the youth club. He had come out a year before. Daniel is studying English and political science and wants to become a teacher. "I found out pretty late," says the 21-year-old, laughing about his coming-out. "It took me longer than most people." The Rosekids was the first place where he knew he would meet other gay people. He came alone to the group. "Normally, I'm not the type to do something like that." Although Generation Z is tolerant of other sexual orientations, coming out is still difficult for many people today. "It took me a long time to come out," says Julien. While he never worried that his family would not accept him, "I couldn't accept myself." During the period of uncertainty before coming out, queer teenagers often have few people to turn to in order to talk about their feelings. Many hesitate to tell their parents or other adults, in large part because they fear rejection. Most parents still have problems coping with the sexuality of their children when they come out. Instead, queer teenagers usually confide in friends, classmates or siblings. Young people who are extremely afraid to come out often experience high levels of depression, anxiety disorders or even suicidal tendencies.

"At first I was afraid to come here," Julien says about his first visit to the Rosekids. After a successful coming-out, Julien talked about it with his family. "Everyone said, 'Why don't you go, what could possibly happen?' I was super nervous the first day." But everything turned out fine. Julien spent the evening chatting with different people and kept going back. Now he knows most of the people in the group. Julien wears his blonde hair short and is dressed in beige pants and a brown turtleneck – the real intellectual type. The 19-year-old from France is studying cultural anthropology and cognitive science in Freiburg. He had many pre-judices before he joined the Rosekids, he says today. "I still had this image of the LGBT community as very colourful and extroverted. And I thought, that's not me at all. Then I came here and saw, 'They're people just like you, and you've got a place among them.'"

"Admitting a part of your identity that you've ignored for so long gives you self-confidence," says Daniel. After coming out, many say they had always known they were gay. "This is a conversation I should have had with myself. Until I was 18, I always thought, 'If I was gay, I'd surely know,'" he says, smiling about the irony. Queer teenagers find their first partners very much the same way as their heterosexual friends do, but usually need more time. The process of coming out often takes years: Initial feelings of difference lead to a search for one's own identity and finally acceptance of oneself. When Markus experienced what he calls his "inner coming-out," his first reaction was: "Holy shit, what are you going to do now?"

Despite growing social acceptance, the knowledge of having a sexual identity different from most of their peers often causes psychological and social issues. Many fear negative and defensive reactions from their surroundings, and some are pushed into the role of social outsider by their peers – during an often agonising phase of self-reflection – because they are different from the majority and do not behave as expected.

Most of all, Julien missed having role models. "I had hardly any opportunity to think about gender norms and sexuality beforehand, so I was pretty lost." He had to meet other gay people to feel normal. While there are at least some public role models gay male teenagers can refer to when discovering their sexuality, gay girls find themselves even more left alone in their coming-out. Today, Julien is surprised by himself. "I never thought I'd go to the Christopher Street Day parade and dance on a float," he says with a laugh. "This feeling of belonging to a community is very liberating." Like many others, coming out has allowed him to be more open – with himself and others. Daniel met his first boyfriend in a chat room while playing computer games. Conversation during the game turned into conversation after the game, and Daniel spontaneously booked a flight to London. "I would never have done anything like that in the past," he says, still a little surprised.

At the Sophie Scholl School in Berlin, students should have more than enough role models to guide them through their coming-out process with self-confidence. The school is in the district of Schöneberg, a centre of gay life in the capital. "Homosexuality has never been an issue here, if only because about 50 percent of my male colleagues are gay," says Juliane Westphal, the head teacher.

Nonetheless, the school has still increased its efforts in recent years to help students to come to terms with their sexuality. In the media library's diversity section, students can check out books on the topic anonymously. They can also pick up the books outside the library, if desired, so that nobody sees them.

This new tolerance does not seem to be limited to the big city either. "It wouldn't be a problem, especially in our class," says Erin, when asked how class 9c in Giessen, a city of 90,000 in the middle of

Germany, would react to a coming-out. "The majority would be sup-portive." "But we've never had that happen yet," objects her classmate Pia. "Nope, never before," says Erin with a smile. "But we'll see what happens in the future. You never know."

Notes

1 Schneekloth and Albert 2019, p. 86.
2 Wolfert and Quenzel 2019, p. 143.
3 Wolfert and Quenzel 2019, p. 140.
4 Wolfert and Quenzel 2019, p. 141.
5 Wolfert and Quenzel 2019, p. 138.
6 Wolfert and Quenzel 2019, p. 138.
7 Wolfert and Quenzel 2019, p. 139.
8 Wolfert and Quenzel 2019, p. 214.
9 Statistisches Bundesamt 2020.
10 Office of National Statistics (ONS) 2019.
11 Wolfert and Quenzel 2019, p. 147.
12 YouGov 2018.
13 Quenzel and Hurrelmann 2012.
14 Leven at al. 2019a, p. 189.
15 Illouz 2019, p. 102.

Chapter 12

Stuck between the climate crisis and the coronavirus pandemic

Politicised for life

"We are young, we are here, we want a future without fear!"

Generation Z is the first post-war generation in German history to be forced once again to confront an existential threat to its future. But as much as the climate crisis threatens their fundamental existence and livelihoods, the fact that they have taken up the fight is likely to be one of the best things that could have happened to them. Young people who become political often remain so for a lifetime. In Germany, as in many other European countries, almost a third of them have become involved in environmental initiatives, most of them in the Fridays for Future movement sparked by Greta Thunberg, transforming one segment of their generation into a veritable "Generation Greta."

Gen Z's formative years were shaped by a long period of economic growth, after the effects of the global financial crisis, which peaked in 2007–2008, subsided. In Central and Northern European countries, that period of uncertainty gave way to an economic boom that would have continued until today, were it not for the coronavirus pandemic. A good education and access to a wide range of information via digital platforms and online media have turned Generation Z into a political powerhouse. By judging the state of the world through the lens of their own futures, they have taken on the greatest threat to their existence: the climate crisis.

But just as this generation was about to finish school, apprenticeships or a first university degree and enter the working world, the coronavirus pandemic hit. The longer it continues, the more this global health crisis will erode the professional and economic prospects of Gen Zers and exacerbate existing divisions within their generation. In addition to the politically active Gretas, there is a large group of socially disadvantaged and marginalised young people who are increasingly susceptible to right-wing populist political ideas. While nearly all of Gen Z will feel the impact of the coronavirus pandemic and the economic downturn it has caused, the disadvantaged members of this generation will suffer much more than those with greater social capital. Generation Z is thus caught between a climate crisis and a health crisis. Their activism was put to an abrupt halt by the lockdown and new health measures. After convincing hundreds of thousands to take to the streets, posting protest signs and memes on social media seems toothless in comparison.

That does not mean, however, that they will give up. This type of politicisation usually lasts a lifetime. With Fridays for Future, Gen Z has gained a crucial platform and public authority to have their say about the vital necessity of a carbon-neutral transformation of European society – regardless of how long it takes to get the pandemic and its aftereffects under control. The reality of the climate crisis has been known among scientists and lay people for decades, but European governments have ignored the consequences for far too long. The part of the younger generation we call "Generation Greta" has revealed this hypocrisy; tens of thousands of young people have taken to the streets to make adults aware of the dimensions of this crisis.

Public protests seldom achieve the exact aims that people hit the streets for. Just think of the student protesters in the late 1960s. It was no different with the anti-nuclear movement or the protests that led to the fall of the Berlin Wall. Nonetheless, each of these movements sparked long-term processes that permanently changed German society and reverberated across international borders.

Fridays for Future, FFF for short, has already succeeded in putting climate policy at the top of the political agenda – not only in Berlin but also in Brussels. This movement of young people, many of them even still in primary school, impressed its elders with its passion, organisational skills and clear agenda. A difficult feat, since their core message is extremely difficult to swallow: To avert the climate crisis, everyone must radically change their way of life. This core message is repeated relentlessly, even in pandemic times.

The health crisis is an acute danger and a burden that demands discipline and restraint from everyone, but it will subside with time. In contrast, the climate crisis is a long-term threat that can only be overcome through an intergenerational effort that needs to continue for decades.

Fighting the climate crisis is just the beginning

In the coming years, a new political force will most likely emerge from the inner circle of FFF activists. With their political talent widely on display in their fight against the climate crisis, they will continue to air their concerns in the public sphere and make themselves heard. Barely old enough to graduate from secondary school, these young activists have managed to break down complicated issues in a way that makes them accessible to broad sections of the population. Their movement has thus turned them into political professionals. They have learned to organise demonstrations for tens of thousands of people, devise creative means of protest and forge alliances with other organisations. And above all, they are professionals in spreading their message in the media. While the forms their protest takes will change over the years, their activism will remain steadfast.

Fighting the climate crisis is only the beginning for this generation. If environmentalism is taken seriously as policy, then Fridays for Future does in fact have a much wider political mandate than simply advocating for carbon-neutral regulations. Energy and transport policy, a reimagination of industrial agriculture towards sustainability, ending food insecurity, large-scale redevelopment of the construction industry, new supply chains, a carbon-neutral economy and, not least, the reorganisation of urban mobility – climate policy has an impact on all areas of life in our complex contemporary societies.

The activists within Generation Z have also learned to translate their ideas into action. They are pioneers when it comes to nutrition: Significantly more teenagers and young adults than their parents and grandparents are vegetarian or vegan. Food production causes a third of all greenhouse gases and consumes 70 percent of global drinking water; meat production consumes significantly more resources than other types of sustenance. Setting the right course here can make a big difference.

The same applies to mobility and the fashion industry. Here too, members of the younger generation are the ones paying particular attention to ending the practices of fast fashion, by advocating for fair conditions, safe working environments and minimising clothing production's ecological footprint. Moreover, Generation Z has also shown that they are ready to shape the digital future. They are pushing for modern forms of learning in schools, and act as digital innovators in the workplace.

With their movement, the Gretas among Gen Z have managed to motivate their parents and grandparents to begin adjusting their lifestyles. Some parents have stopped buying single-use plastic containers; some now go on vacation by train instead of flying; some have decided on a smaller new family car than originally planned; others have cut back on their meat consumption. The private sphere has become political again, and at many dinner tables, Generation Z sets the agenda. Young people use their close relationship with their parents to bring about small changes while pushing for new policies on the streets.

This distinguishes them from Generation Y, the millennials, who were born before the turn of the millennium and are now in their 20s and early 30s. For the most part, Gen Yers were concerned with themselves, their education and professional careers – or, more pointedly, they are the 'ego-tacticians.' The members of today's youngest generation, the post-millennials, are different: They see themselves as existentially threatened by the climate crisis and consider it their mission to take active steps to combat it. They are prepared to take responsibility for necessary political changes but also feel that they are running up against a wall of ignorance and inaction. In response, they are constantly developing new, unexpected and provocative ways to draw attention to their concerns, consistently placing ever greater pressure on politicians to act.

From ego-tacticians to eco-tacticians

The post-millennials are not ego-tacticians, but eco-tacticians who are constantly speaking out in public and creating ever new approaches to fighting for a radical change in national and international climate policy. If they stick to it, they could even become eco-strategists.

The coronavirus pandemic has made their fight much more difficult. On the one hand, the health crisis has proven all those people wrong who declared that the changes needed to prevent the climate crisis from destroying our planet were too radical. One year into the pandemic, no one can argue anymore that travelling less, reducing commutes and drastically changing our way of life is impossible. On the other hand, fighting the virus and dealing with the economic impact of the pandemic has taken a significant toll on many of those whose resources and attention spans are needed to fight the climate crisis.

Despite the lockdowns and public health measures needed under pandemic conditions, the Gretas among Gen Zers will not disappear from public view. They are much better prepared for the climate crisis than the boomers and Generation X. Growing up in times of society-wide upheaval has taught them to be agile and flexible. They already know what it means to adapt when globalisation and digitalisation sweep away existing structures and certainties. In response, they have developed a strong capacity for self-control and self-discipline that enables them to lead a largely autonomous life. This attitude will be crucial for survival.

As adolescents, young people are only just setting the course toward their futures; this gives them the chance to choose a more climate-friendly life from the start. A job that involves commuting long-distance every day? A suburban house with no access to public transportation? Knowing that CO_2 emissions will come at a price in the long run, the younger generation will think twice when making such decisions.

In their book *On the End of the Climate Crisis*, Luisa Neubauer and Alexander Repenning outline their vision of a world without microplastics in toothpaste, one with regional produce at fair prices for consumers and farmers, safe bicycle routes on the streets and public transport for everyone. In their vision for the future, a railway ticket does not cost more than 25 euros, repair cafes ensure the reusability of electrical appliances, companies must submit a public interest balance sheet with their tax returns, the work week has been reduced to 30 hours, and an unconditional basic income supports society as a whole. In addition, the carbon-neutral reorganisation of society is financed by a climate fund made up of a CO_2 tax, a one-time capital levy and a levy for renewable energy. Instead of banning wind turbines near residential areas, towns will receive a cut of the profit, which will exponentially accelerate the expansion of wind energy. It goes without saying that every building will have climate-friendly insulation installed.[1]

A new way of life

As this vision of the future shows, the young generation has clear ideas. Greta Thunberg speaks of herself as a child who had to grow up quickly because of the childish refusal of adults to take responsibility. The environmental movement she initiated heralded the beginning of a great experiment, writes Bernd Ulrich in the German weekly *Die Zeit*, namely the reimagination of Western democracy based on a liberal model of society that does not exploit natural resources.

The Gretas among Generation Z want a new social contract, and the prospect of material abundance will not seduce them into putting up with living in a shattered ecosystem. Working without the opportunity to participate in designing a company's business model has become unacceptable for them. They seek fulfilment at work instead of wealth and want to be involved in shaping society, instead of buying happiness in the form of plastics and fast fashion. They know that existing forms of capitalism have pushed the planet to its limits and that they will have to live with the resulting uncertainties. For the politically active Generation Zers, the fight against climate change is the starting point for a new way of life. As illustrated throughout this book, they have a clear vision of how this can be implemented.

Generation Z knows who they can count on. Even though Fridays for Future understands the climate crisis as a question of justice between young and old, young people today want to join forces with their parents and grandparents. The close relationship within the family strengthens their political clout, cogency and impact – and provides them with personal support in uncertain times.

Generation Z will not wait for political parties to catch up. As political as they may be, the traditional political parties that cater mainly to the older generations do not impress Gen Zers. They believe in democracy but feel alienated from a parliamentary system they see as beset by lobbyists and compromise. With the clout of their movement behind them, they have brought climate change from the streets to the centre of political debate far more quickly and effectively than the youth wings of the established parties could ever have done. At the same time, their protests continue to put external pressure on all political parties.

Generation Z is ready to debate about the path forward. For decades, politicians have attempted to win elections by appealing to the centre. For this generation, that no longer works – they are looking at different options and are ready to endure the ambiguities and contradictions that come with that. In the future, they could also be open to new political forces that offer more constructive visions for the future. After all, if our society is to survive the climate crisis and flourish, it will take a range of competing ideas to get there.

Generation Z thinks digitally. They use online forms of media not only for personal communication, but also to organise and coordinate their activism. Through their command of the digital sphere, they will have their say about the future. Their scepticism about digital media giants such as Google and Facebook, coupled with their commitment to a free internet, demonstrates how this is a generation that wants to play an active role in shaping the future of the global web in a way that works for them, not for companies like Apple or Amazon.

Generation Z wants to learn interactively. Lifelong learning is not a buzzword for them, but an inevitable reality. They will join the workforce at a time in which digitalisation and artificial intelligence are changing job descriptions faster than they can get their degrees. Their desire to learn more than just factual information at school – more digital skills, greater knowledge about the dangers of the internet and better social skills – makes them a force to be reckoned with. Their critiques of school as an institution show that they understand what it takes to be successful in their careers and in their lives as a whole.

Generation Z wants to work independently. They grew up believing in their freedom of choice to do what they wanted with their professional lives. With baby boomers retiring from the workforce and creating a huge shortage of skilled workers, their prospects seemed endless – at least until the coronavirus crisis hit. At the same time, the pandemic will drive change, especially in terms of digitalisation, and here Generation Zers are simply unbeatable. Instead of fearing digitalisation, they see it as an opportunity, allowing them to succeed under difficult conditions, despite the awareness that digitalisation has the potential to cause quite a few gaps in their resumés.

Generation Z seeks happiness beyond their work lives. Young people today have a much greater scope to define their own identity – including their sexual identity. For the young generation, LGBTQI* has become a household term, but coming out still involves a certain level of insecurity, uncertainty and fear. All in all, the younger generation attaches a great deal of importance to the values that give their lives meaning and ensure a high quality of life. This includes a good standard of living, but also stability, diligence and ambition. In contrast, materialistic desires and values that focus on personal power and self-assertion are diminishing in importance. Gen Z wants to address issues that concern the future, articulate their concerns and make their voices heard.

Women have become the stronger force in Generation Z. The activist segment within Generation Z bears the name of a teenage girl, Greta Thunberg. Girls and young women have become trendsetters when it comes to finding suitable strategies of self-management and personal behaviour. They have set the course for a healthy and environmentally responsible life for themselves, as well as provided help for the socially disadvantaged. They are the ones who are actively looking for innovative ways to balance private and professional life and, above all, to balance having a family and career. They set the tone within the environmental movement and succeed in asserting themselves and their needs against others without resorting to older models of dominance and power. Young men remain more materialistic and focused on power and influence, and they have much greater difficulty coping with the uncertainties and unpredictability inherent in planning for their futures.

These are this generation's reference points for a fulfilling and dedicated life.

Today, adults can no longer claim superiority over young people. Fridays for Future rightly accuses older generations of having neglected the development of reasonable strategies for tacking fundamental problems and instead becoming stuck in lazy and comfortable patterns of consumption. That Generation Zers have embarked on the struggle for a new understanding of a meaningful life is probably the best thing that could have happened to all of us – old, young and everywhere in between. Looking directly at Generation Z, one cannot help but think: If only we had listened to them sooner.

Generation Greta or Generation Covid?

This book, however, has also shown that the active members of Generation Z, the Gretas, are not representative of the entirety of the younger population. In Germany, our case study, they account for about 40 percent at present. In addition, almost 30 percent remain undecided, and more than 30 percent have been left behind. The undecided will somehow succeed – they have kept (or will keep) their options open for how they intend to organise their lives one day. They are opportunistic and adaptable. But when in doubt, most of them will orient themselves towards those who are active and engaged.

Conversely, those left behind will remain insecure and disoriented. The way of life espoused by the Gretas is completely alien to them. They are overwhelmed by educational requirements and behavioural rules in a complex society experiencing such rapid change, and cannot turn to their own parents, many of whom also have difficulty finding their way professionally and socially. Climate change is not their major concern; they are finding it hard enough to navigate their own path in society.

The 2007–2008 global economic crisis revealed just how much major external shocks and events affect different population groups to different extents. The economically and educationally well-off segments of the population will almost invariably succeed in maintaining or even increasing their standard of living despite the challenges of a crisis, whereas those groups who are already socially disadvantaged will continue to suffer under deteriorating conditions. The group in the middle will remain stuck somewhere in between, muddling through until the situation improves. This division of fortunes also applies to the economic and labour market crises triggered by the coronavirus pandemic. Well-situated social groups who live in large flats or single-family houses in well-maintained neighbourhoods are much more able to reduce the risk of infection than those in densely populated, poorer urban areas. In addition, the massive contact restrictions imposed to manage and control the health crisis have a far greater impact on socially disadvantaged groups, many of whom often live in multi-generational arrangements. This is true of every crisis: The weak are invariably harmed the most.

The affluent and well-educated segment of the younger generation – Generation Greta – will always manage to succeed, even under difficult conditions. But the socially disadvantaged could slip into becoming a permanent "Generation Covid." Even during the economic boom times of 2010–2019, these young people struggled at school and had a hard time starting their careers. In the aftermath of the coronavirus pandemic, under considerably more adverse conditions, they are really at risk. Their education came almost to a complete standstill under the lockdown conditions imposed in the pandemic, as schools closed and then re-opened only partially. Contact restrictions made traditional teaching impossible, which meant teachers had to introduce new forms of communication and pedagogy – often on the fly and without sufficient resources. Their parents were unable to cope with the quadruple demands of childcare, supporting online learning at home, managing the household and pursuing their professional activities. Schools with a large ratio of students from educated families have had far greater success working with these new forms of learning, but schools in socially disadvantaged neighbourhoods have performed poorly, with many teachers unable to even maintain contact with the children in their classes. This situation has led to an increase in learning deficits and further aggravated already existing social inequalities.

Ultimately, the historic challenge for Generation Z will entail successfully navigating the now twin crises of climate change and the coronavirus pandemic. Depending on the socio-economic group they belong to, their chances will vary considerably. Yet we can be certain that they will demand to have their say in these and other decisions that affect not just their generation but society as a whole. Youth, as they have so often been in the past, may be among those best positioned to develop creative solutions for society's core issues: building the carbon-neutral future they envision for all of us, and creating equal opportunities for all segments of society and all generations.

Note

1 Neubauer und Repenning 2019, p. 225.

References

Andresen, Sabine, Fegter, Susann, Hurrelmann, Klaus and Schneekloth, Ulrich (Eds.) (2017) *Well-being, Poverty and Justice from a Child's Perspective.* Cham: Springer International Publishing.

Autorengruppe Bildungsberichterstattung (2018) Bielefeld: wbv media.

Children's Commissioner (2018) *Who knows what about me? A Children's Commissioner report into the collection and sharing of children's data.* https://www.chil drenscommissioner.gov.uk/publication/who-knows-what-about-me/.

Eribon, Didier (2009) *Retour à Reims.* Paris: Fayard.

Fraillon, Julian, Ainley, John, Schulz, Wolfram, Friedman, Tim and Duckworth, Daniel (Ed.) (2019) *Preparing for life in a digital world. IEA International Computer and Information Literacy Study 2018 International Report.* IEA.

Fridays for Future (2019) Unsere Forderungen an die Politik, https://fridaysfor future.de/forderungen.

Friedrichs, Julia (2015) *Wir Erben. Was Geld mit Menschen macht.* Berlin: Berlin-Verlag.

Green, Francis and Kynaston, David (2019) Britain's private school problem: it's time to talk. In: *The Guardian*, 13/01/2019.

Guess, Andrew, Nagler, Jonathan and Tucker, Joshua (2019) Less than you think. Prevalence and predictors of fake news dissemination on Facebook. In: *Science Advances* 5(1). doi:10.1126/sciadv.aau4586.

Haunss, Sebastian, Rucht, Dieter, Sommer, Moritz and Zajak, Sabrina (2019) Germany. In: Mattias Wahlström, Piotr Kocyba, Michiel de Vydt and Joost de Moor (Ed.) *Protest for a future: Composition, mobilization and motives of the participants in Fridays For Future climate protests.* https://www.researchgate. net/publication/334745801.

Herzog, Lisa (2019) *Die Rettung der Arbeit.* Berlin: Hanser.

Hurrelmann, Klaus and Albrecht, Erik (2014) *Die heimlichen Revolutionäre. Wie die Generation Y unsere Welt verändert.* Weinheim: Beltz.

Hurrelmann, Klaus and Bauer, Ullrich (2018) *Socialisation during the life course.* London: Routledge.

Hurrelmann, Klaus and Quenzel, Gudrun (2013) Lost in transition. Status insecurity and inconsistency as hallmarks of modern adolescence. *International Journal of Adolescence and Youth* 15, 261–270.

Hurrelmann, Klaus and Quenzel, Gudrun (2019) *Developmental tasks in adolescence*. London: Routledge.

Hurrelmann, Klaus and Richter, Matthias (2020) *Understanding Public Health*. London: Routledge.

Hurrelmann, Klaus, Karch, Heribert and Traxler, Christian (2019) *Jugend, Vorsorge, Finanzen*. Weinheim: Beltz.

Illouz, Eva (2019) *Warum Liebe endet*. Frankfurt: Suhrkamp.

Jugendrat (2020) *Ihr habt keinen Plan, darum machen wir einen!* Munich: Blessing.

Kiselica, Mark S., Benton-Wright, Sheila and Englar-Carlson, Matt (2016) Accentuating positive masculinity: A new foundation for the psychology of boys, men, and masculinity. In: Y. Joel Wong and Stephen R. Wester (Ed.) *APA handbook of men and masculinities*. Washington, DC: American Psychological Association, 123–143.

KMK (2015) *Bildung in der digitalen Welt*. Bonn: KMK.

Köcher, Renate, Sommer, Michael and Hurrelmann, Klaus (2019) *Kinder der Einheit. Die McDonald's Ausbildungsstudie*. Düsseldorf: Castenow.

Leven, Ingo, Hurrelmann, Klaus and Quenzel, Gudrun (2019a) Beruf und Karriere. In: *Jugend 2019. Shell Jugendstudie*. Weinheim: Beltz, pp. 187–212.

Leven, Ingo, Quenzel, Gudrun and Hurrelmann, Klaus (2019b) Bildung. In: *Jugend 2019. Shell Jugendstudie*. Weinheim: Beltz, pp. 163–186.

Lobo, Sascha (2019) *Realitätsschock. Zehn Lehren aus der Gegenwart*. Cologne: Kiepenheuer & Witsch.

Mannheim, Karl (1970) The Problem of Generations. *Psychoanalytic Review* 57(3), 378–404.

mpfs (2020) JIM-Studie. Basisuntersuchung zum Medienumgang 12- bis 19-Jähriger. https://www.mpfs.de/studien/jim-studie.

Neubauer, Luisa-Marie (2020) Make the climate a priority again. https://www.npr.org/2020/07/03/885644410/.

Neubauer, Luisa-Marie and Repenning, Alexander (2019) *Vom Ende der Klimakrise. Eine Geschichte unserer Zukunft*. Stuttgart: Tropen.

OECD (2018) *Equity in Education*. Paris: OECD.

Office of National Statistics (ONS) (2019) Families and the labour market, UK. https://www.ons.gov.uk/employmentandlabourmarket/peopleinwork/emp loymentandemployeetypes/articles/familiesandthelabourmarketengland/2019.

Pereira, Fabiano Souza, Bevilacqua, Guilherme Guimarães, Coimbra, Danilo Reis, Andrade, Alexandro (2020) Impact of Problematic Smartphone Use on Mental Health of Adolescent Students. *Cyberpsychology, Behavior and Social Networking* 23(9), 619–626. doi:10.1089/cyber.2019.0257.

Piketty, Thomas (2014) *Capital in the Twenty-First Century*. Cambridge: Harvard University Press.

Quenzel, Gudrun and Hurrelmann, Klaus (2012) The growing gender gap in education. *International Journal of Adolescence and Youth* 18(2), 69–84.

Reckwitz, Andreas (2018) *Die Gesellschaft der Singularitäten. Zum Strukturwandel der Moderne*. Berlin: Suhrkamp.

Rezo (2019) Die Zerstörung der CDU. https://www.youtube.com/watch?v=4Y1lZQsyuSQ.

Schelsky, Helmut (1963) *Die skeptische Generation*. Düsseldorf: Diederichs.

Schneekloth, Ulrich and Albert, Mathias (2019) Jugend und Politik. In: *Jugend 2019. Shell Jugendstudie*. Weinheim: Beltz, p. 47–102.

Seabrook, John (2019) The Next Word. Where will predictive text take us? In: *The New Yorker*, 14/10/2019.

Seemiller, Corey and Grace, Meghan (2017) Generation Z. Educating and Engaging the Next Generation of Students. In: *About Campus* 22(3), 21–26. doi:10.1002/abc.21293.

Seemiller, Corey and Grace, Meghan (2019) *Generation Z. A century in the making*. London: Routledge.

Social Mobility Commission (2019) *State of the nation 2018–2019. Social mobility in Great Britain*. London: Social Mobility Commission.

SRzG Stiftung für die Rechte zukünftiger Generationen (2015) Der Generationen-Soli. Stuttgart: SRzG.

Statistisches Bundesamt (2020) Gut sechs von zehn jungen Erwachsenen leben noch bei den Eltern. https://www.destatis.de/DE/Presse/Pressemitteilungen/Zahl-der-Woche/2016/PD16_47_p002.html.

Stiglic, Neza and Viner, Russell M. (2019) Effects of screentime on the health and well-being of children and adolescents. A systematic review of reviews. *BMJ Open*, doi:10.1136/bmjopen-2018-023191.

SZ (2019) "Ich habe Papa schon oft gesagt, dass ich sein Handy nicht mag." In: *SZ Magazin*, 30/10/2019 (44).

Thunberg, Greta (2019) *No one is too small to make a difference*. New York: Penguin Books.

Twenge, Joan M. (2017a) *iGen*. New York: Simon & Schuster.

Twenge, Joan M. (2017b) Have smartphones destroyed a generation? *Atlantic*. Available at https://www.theatlantic.com/amp/article/534198.

Wahlström, Mattias, Sommer, Moritz, Kocyba, Piotr, Vydt, Michiel de, Moor, Joost de and Davies, Stephen (2019) Fridays For Future: a new generation of climate activism. In: Mattias Wahlström, Piotr Kocyba, Michiel de Vydt and Joost de Moor (Ed.) *Protest for a future: Composition, mobilization and motives of the participants in Fridays For Future climate protests*. https://gup.ub.gu.se/publication/283193..

Wilkinson, Richard G. and Pickett, Kate (2011) *Spirit level. Why equality is better for everyone*. London: Penguin Books.

Wolfert, Sabine and Quenzel, Gudrun (2019) Vielfalt jugendlicher Lebenswelten. In: *Jugend 2019. Shell Jugendstudie*. Weinheim: Beltz, pp. 133–162.

Wolfert, Sabine and Leven, Ingo (2019) Freizeitgestaltung und Internetnutzung. In: *Jugend 2019. Shell Jugendstudie*. Weinheim: Beltz, pp. 213–246.

YouGov (2019) Four in ten men in heterosexual relationships feel a responsibility to be the "main breadwinner". Available at https://yougov.co.uk/topics/relationships/articles-reports/2018/11/01/four-ten-men-heterosexual-relationships-feel-respo.

Index

For Product Safety Concerns and Information please contact our EU
representative GPSR@taylorandfrancis.com
Taylor & Francis Verlag GmbH, Kaufingerstraße 24, 80331 München, Germany

www.ingramcontent.com/pod-product-compliance
Lightning Source LLC
Chambersburg PA
CBHW050717280326
41926CB00088B/3084